SHOW ME HOW TO
SURVIVE

SHOW ME HOW

TO SURVIVE

THE HANDBOOK FOR THE MODERN HERO

JOSEPH PRED

OUTDOORLIFE

home safety

first aid

wilderness skills

◆ prevail

a note from joseph

167 ▷ battle a pit bull

As an emergency manager, I've advised individuals and organizations on everything from minor problems such as stopping a nosebleed (#95) to large-scale environmental challenges, like avoiding an avalanche (#136). While writing this book, I was lucky to be able to draw on my day-to-day professional experience with life-saving procedures like CPR (#56), as well as my personal interest in the challenges in the great outdoors, such as cleaning up an oil spill (#107) . . . and a few problems I hope to never have to deal with, like repelling an angry pit bull (#167). Through my research in preparing this book, I learned a few new things that may prove useful one day, such as keeping pets safe after a disaster (#12), how to fight a shark (#165), or how to build a flood barrier with sandbags (#15). In my line of work, you can never be too prepared, so although I hope no one will ever need them, I've also included instructions for saving a child from a coyote (#149) and disarming a shooter (#45). Stay safe out there!

95 stop a nosebleed

45 disarm a shooter

To be truly prepared for any emergency, it's best to start getting ready now, before you find yourself face-to-face with a mountain lion.

get jungle savvy 151

Start by packing a go bag (a kit containing everything you'd need to get by for 48 hours in an emergency). Include personal items like ID, food, medicine, tools like a flashlight and knife, and other handy survival items like a dust mask, a radio (with extra batteries), and a list of emergency contact numbers.

Now that you have your physical needs handled, work on your brain by practicing "situational awareness." Stay attentive to your surroundings, your wellbeing, the presence of others, and possible dangers or threats. It isn't about looking for problems, it's about avoiding becoming complacent and making mistakes as a result.

For instance, imagine yourself hiking through an unfamiliar jungle (#151). Without worrying or panicking, stay aware of whether anyone in your party is tired, hungry, or injured. Focus on the path ahead of you, while keeping a relaxed state of awareness about your surroundings—watching for predators, poisonous plants, and insects.

A positive, relaxed, open mindset also saves lives in the field. Someone with a negative outlook might panic or give up when faced with a swimmer in trouble (#104), but a person who focuses on solutions will quickly scan the beach for a rescue aid and jump in the water.

Ready for an adventure? Just keep these basic tenets of great rescue work in mind as you read through the book and you'll be a hero in no time!

rescue a swimmer in trouble 104

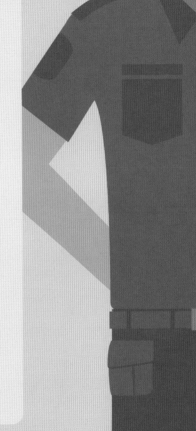

how to use this book

In the pages that follow, virtually every piece of essential information is presented graphically. In most cases the pictures do, indeed, tell the whole story. In some cases though, you'll need a little extra information to get it done right. Here's how we present those facts.

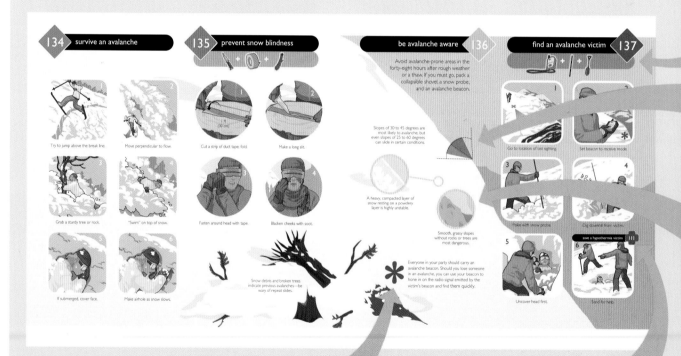

MORE INFORMATION Follow the * symbol to learn more about the how and why of the given step.

CROSS-REFERENCES When one activity just leads to another, we'll point it out. Follow the links for related or interesting information.

save a hypothermia victim 111

TOOLS Everything you'll need to perform an activity appears in the toolbars. Having a hard time deciphering an item? Turn to the tools glossary in the back of the book.

MATH When measurements matter, find them right in the box. Handy "angle" icons help you do it from the right angle.

 1 lb (450 g)   ½ in (1.25 cm)

ZOOMS These little circles zoom in on a step's important details, or depict the step's crucial "don'ts."

ICON GUIDE Throughout the book, handy icons show you just how it's done. Here are the icons you'll encounter.

 Check out the timer to learn how much time a relatively short task takes.

 The calendar shows how many days, weeks, or months an activity requires.

 Look to the thermometer to learn the temperature needed for a given action.

 Repeat the depicted action the designated number of times.

 The phone icon lets you know when it's time to call for professional medical help.

 Danger! Avoid this if you're not trained. (Or if you don't want to get into trouble!)

A NOTE TO READERS The depictions in this book are presented for entertainment value only. Please keep the following in mind:

- RISKY ACTIVITIES Certain activities in this book are not just risky but downright nutty (like #169, for example). Before attempting any new activity, make sure you are aware of your own limitations and have adequately researched all applicable risks.

- PROFESSIONAL ADVICE While every item has been carefully researched, this book is not intended to replace professional advice or training of a medical, architectural, sartorial, culinary, athletic, or therapeutic nature—or any other professional advice, for that matter.

- PHYSICAL AND HEALTH-RELATED ACTIVITIES Be sure to consult a physician before attempting any activity involving physical exertion, particularly if you have a condition that could impair or limit your ability to engage in such an activity. Or if you don't want to look silly (see #75).

- ADULT CONTENT The activities in this book are intended for adults only. Some of them are probably unwise even for adults; use your common sense and discretion (if, for instance, you plan to attempt #39).

- BREAKING THE LAW The information in this book should not be used to break any applicable law or regulation. In other words, just don't even think about trying #60. Ever.

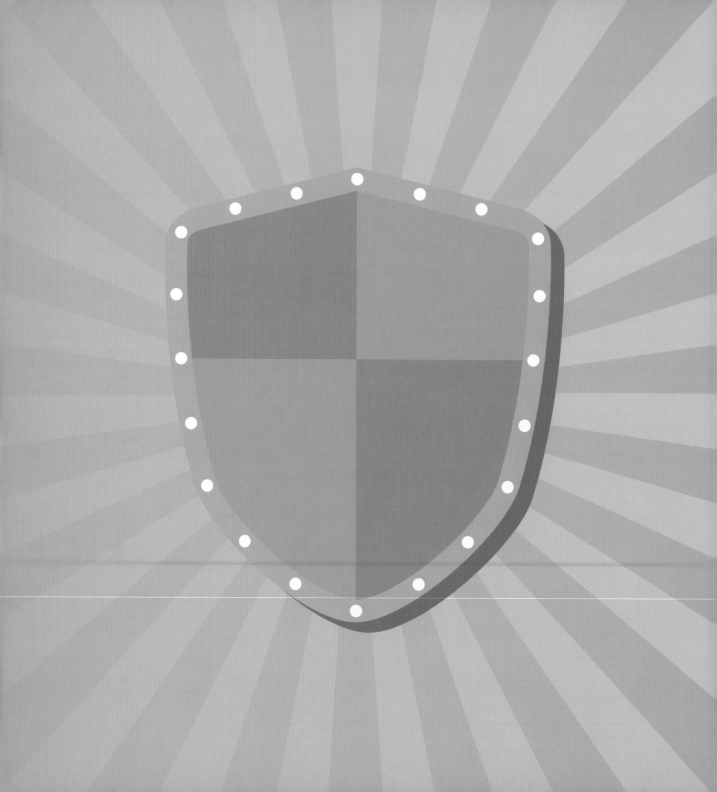

It doesn't take a rocket scientist to figure out that failing to plan is planning to fail. It's impossible to anticipate every problem that may be thrown your way, but it only takes a little effort to figure out the likely challenges you could be facing. For the ones you can't anticipate, you can create general plans and resources that are flexible. Of course, the most flexible tool you have available is your reasoning, so be sure to keep a positive attitude and an open mind. Both of those mentalities will be valuable resources to help you out when you need it most.

protect

navigate the mean streets

Whether you're in the city walking to dinner or in a jungle trying to avoid becoming dinner, situational awareness is a vital survival skill. To start practicing it, adopt an awareness of your surroundings and possible threats and hazards.

Buddy up! There's safety in numbers.

If you feel threatened, call the police.

Avoid using cash machines in shady areas.

Pay attention! Don't use your cell phone or tune out your surroundings.

Don't let strangers' questions or remarks distract you.

Always have your keys at hand, and sling your bag across your body.

Being followed? Try crossing the street or moving to a more crowded place.

stay safe in the wilderness

2

Tell a friend your plans.

Dress appropriately.

Bring an emergency kit.

Monitor weather conditions.

Know your route.

148 fend off a mountain lion

Be aware of animals.

Avoid poisons and venoms.

Rest; avoid overexertion.

be prepared at the office

3

Be aware of possible exits.

Attend safety trainings.

Report issues promptly.

Pack a go bag and shoes.

+ +

Discuss possible local hazards.

Practice appropriate responses.

Have an out-of-state contact person.

Add emergency numbers to family phones.

Set a meeting place in case of separation.

Teach kids to trust emergency workers.

An out-of-state friend or relative can relay information between members of your family if you're separated during an emergency. Make sure everyone has that person's phone number and knows to check in.

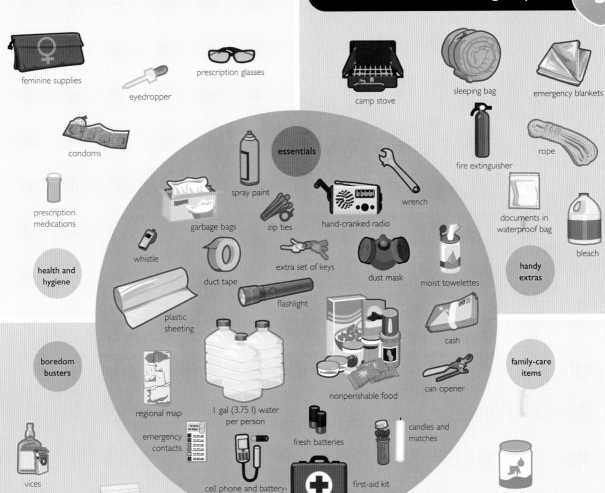

essentials

feminine supplies

eyedropper

prescription glasses

condoms

prescription
medications

spray paint

garbage bags

zip ties

hand-cranked radio

wrench

whistle

extra set of keys

dust mask

moist towelettes

duct tape

flashlight

plastic
sheeting

cash

nonperishable food

can opener

regional map

1 gal (3.75 l) water
per person

candles and
matches

emergency
contacts

fresh batteries

cell phone and battery-
powered charger

first-aid kit

health and
hygiene

handy
extras

bleach

documents in
waterproof bag

camp stove

sleeping bag

emergency blankets

fire extinguisher

rope

boredom
busters

family-care
items

vices

dice

paper and pen

cards

books

baby wipes

baby formula

diapers

pet food

stock a bunker

Nuclear war may be passé, but a well-appointed underground bunker will never go out of style.

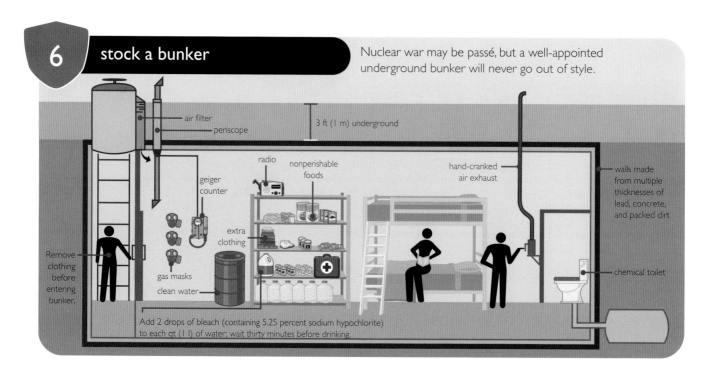

air filter
periscope
3 ft (1 m) underground
radio
nonperishable foods
hand-cranked air exhaust
walls made from multiple thicknesses of lead, concrete, and packed dirt
geiger counter
extra clothing
Remove clothing before entering bunker.
gas masks
clean water
chemical toilet
Add 2 drops of bleach (containing 5.25 percent sodium hypochlorite) to each qt (1 l) of water; wait thirty minutes before drinking.

prepare a flood dinghy

If you live in a flood-prone area, be ready to make a quick escape in a stocked dinghy, launched from an upper floor.

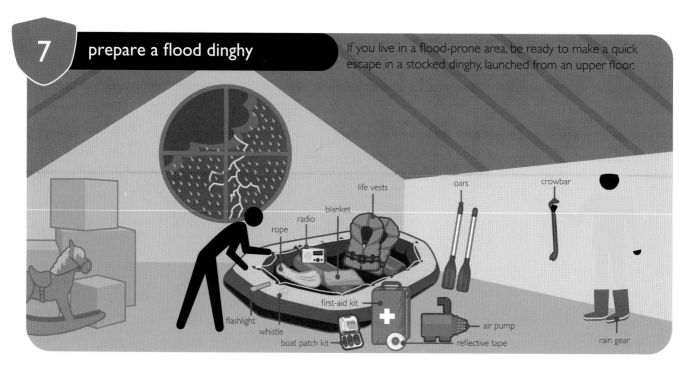

life vests
oars
crowbar
blanket
radio
rope
flashlight
whistle
boat patch kit
first-aid kit
air pump
reflective tape
rain gear

Nervous about home invaders? Stay safe in the comfort of your own home with a custom-built panic room.

Soundproof the walls and reinforce them with steel.

security cameras

security monitor

intercom

gas masks

buried phone line

toilet

water and nonperishable food

ventilated generator

Hide the entrance behind a bookcase or in a closet.

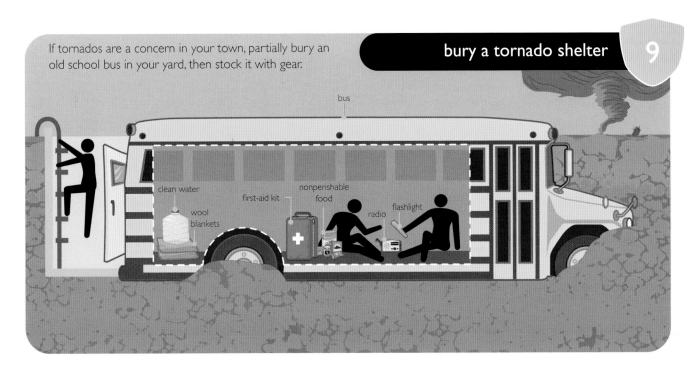

If tornados are a concern in your town, partially bury an old school bus in your yard, then stock it with gear.

bus

clean water

first-aid kit

nonperishable food

wool blankets

radio

flashlight

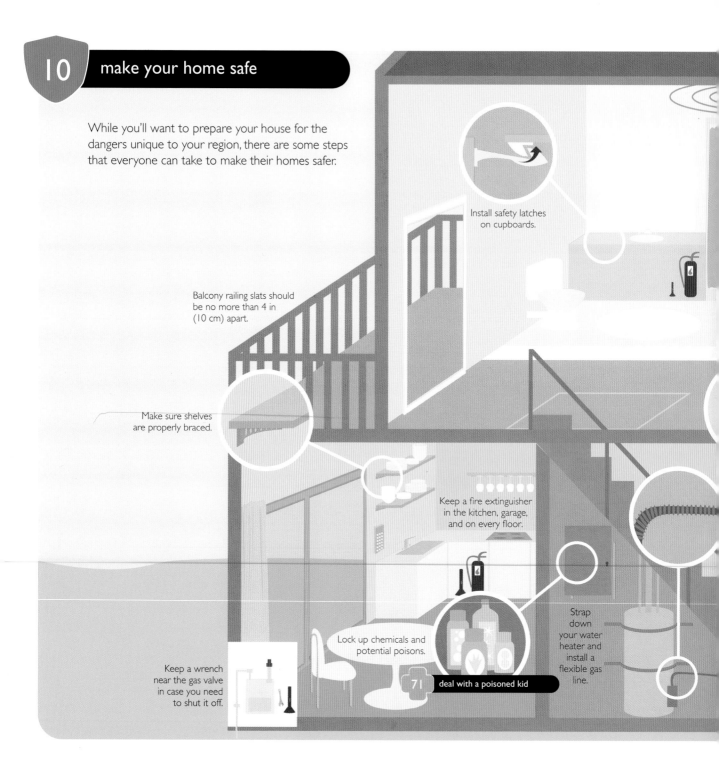

While you'll want to prepare your house for the dangers unique to your region, there are some steps that everyone can take to make their homes safer.

Install safety latches on cupboards.

Balcony railing slats should be no more than 4 in (10 cm) apart.

Make sure shelves are properly braced.

Keep a fire extinguisher in the kitchen, garage, and on every floor.

Lock up chemicals and potential poisons.

Strap down your water heater and install a flexible gas line.

Keep a wrench near the gas valve in case you need to shut it off.

71 deal with a poisoned kid

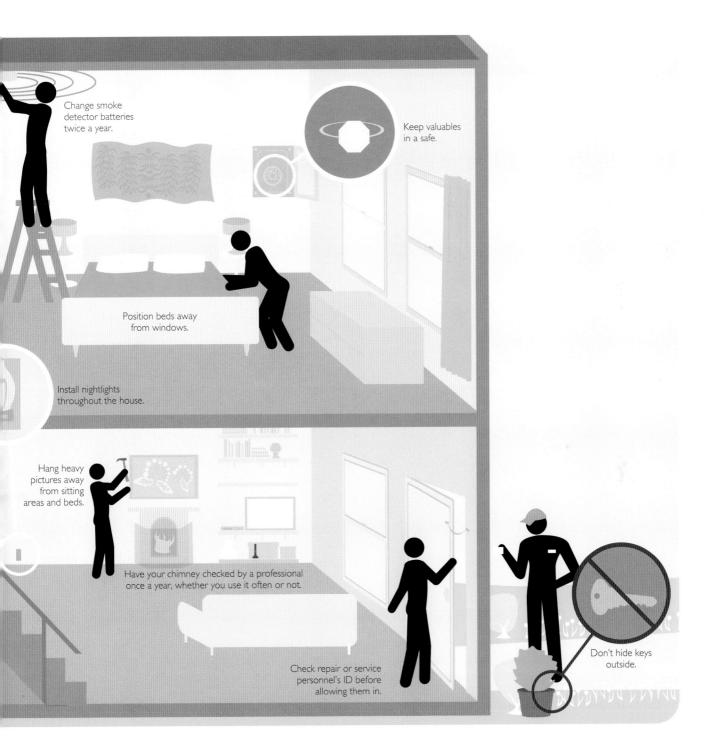

Change smoke detector batteries twice a year.

Keep valuables in a safe.

Position beds away from windows.

Install nightlights throughout the house.

Hang heavy pictures away from sitting areas and beds.

Have your chimney checked by a professional once a year, whether you use it often or not.

Check repair or service personnel's ID before allowing them in.

Don't hide keys outside.

11 prepare your pet

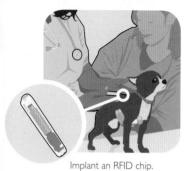

Implant an RFID chip.

Attach ID tags to collar.

Keep a photo in your wallet.

Have pet's go bag packed.

12 keep pets safe after a disaster

Separate pets.

Secure them in the house.

If you must evacuate your home without taking your pets along, take these steps to ensure their safety until rescuers arrive.

101 rescue a cat up a tree

If you are able to evacuate with your pets, keep them on a leash, even if you don't normally.

Leave plenty of food, water.

Leave a note for rescuers.

2 cats inside

Many animals behave strangely before a disaster like a tsunami or an earthquake. Take care if your pet is acting oddly, or if you see any of these behaviors.

Hoofed animals may huddle together in open areas.

Farm animals may pace or refuse to be tied or led into their barns.

Spiders and ants move indoors.

Rodents who live inside will flee (and outdoor rodents may try to get in).

Confined animals, like those in the zoo, may try to escape.

Hibernating animals will wake early and leave their dens.

be bear aware 147

Birds will push eggs from their nests.

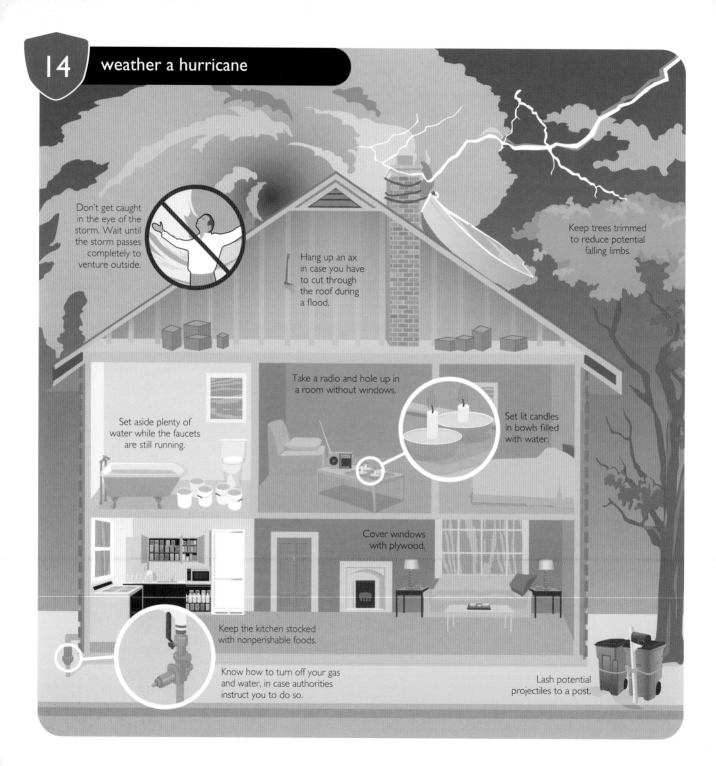

Don't get caught in the eye of the storm. Wait until the storm passes completely to venture outside.

Hang up an ax in case you have to cut through the roof during a flood.

Keep trees trimmed to reduce potential falling limbs.

Take a radio and hole up in a room without windows.

Set lit candles in bowls filled with water.

Set aside plenty of water while the faucets are still running.

Cover windows with plywood.

Keep the kitchen stocked with nonperishable foods.

Know how to turn off your gas and water, in case authorities instruct you to do so.

Lash potential projectiles to a post.

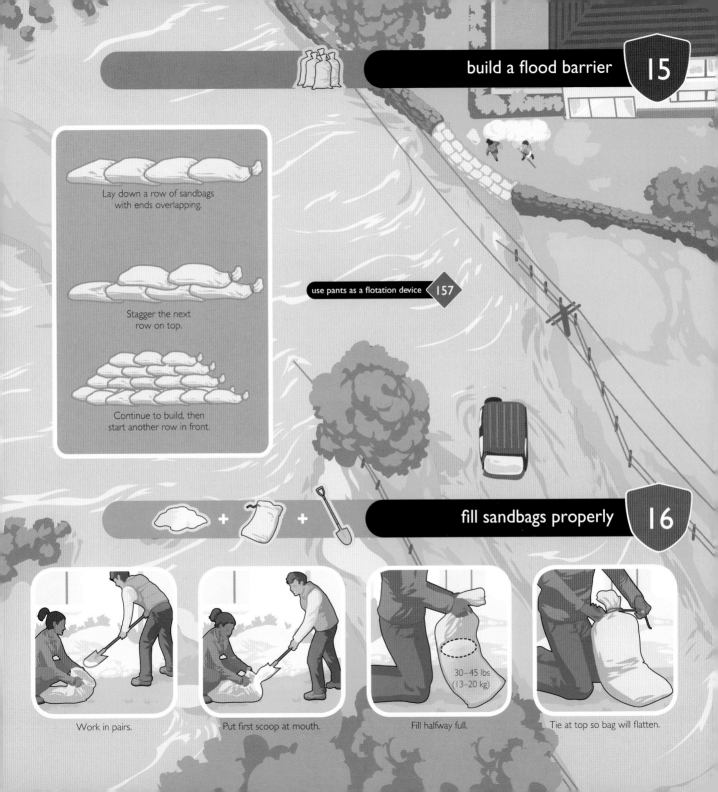

Lay down a row of sandbags with ends overlapping.

Stagger the next row on top.

Continue to build, then start another row in front.

use pants as a flotation device 157

fill sandbags properly 16

30–45 lbs (13–20 kg)

Work in pairs.

Put first scoop at mouth.

Fill halfway full.

Tie at top so bag will flatten.

firescape a yard

Firescaping is a method of designing the space and conditions around your home with fire prevention in mind. If you live in a dry climate, check out these tips.

Clear away low-hanging branches, deadwood, or debris within 30 ft (9 m) of your home.

Don't plant conifers—they contain highly flammable oils and resins.

Grow only fire-resistant plants within 3 ft (1 m) of structures.

Cover bare spaces with stone, mulch, or high-moisture plants.

Keep plants moist all year with drip irrigation.

Store firewood at least 30 ft (9 m) from your home.

fight fire with an extinguisher

Pull pin.

Aim low.

Pull trigger; sweep fire's base.

Monitor for reignition.

Install a spark arrester on your chimney.

Preparation is key to keeping calm during a fire. Practice these basic fire-safety techniques with your family so everyone knows just what to do in an emergency.

Stay low and cover your mouth with a damp cloth.

Have fire-escape ladders on hand near windows.

Check windows often to make sure none are stuck.

Draw up an exit plan that provides two emergency escape routes from each room. Practice it with your household.

Lower kids down first if you must escape through a window.

Keep hallways clear. Clutter can hinder your escape.

Touch each door before opening it. If it feels hot, take a different route.

Don't try to put out a large fire yourself.

Have a meeting place nearby as the endpoint of your escape plan.

Cover external vents with fine metal screen to keep forest fire embers from blowing in.

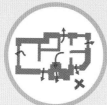

20 prepare for travel

Have your mail held.

Set lights on a timer.

Dispose of perishables.

Lock the windows.

21 stay smart abroad

Copy important documents.

Register with your embassy.

Pack extra meds.

Dress modestly.

Give travel info to a neighbor.

Unplug appliances.

Stop any leaks or drips.

Adjust the thermostat.

Wear a money belt.

Stay sly by silencing ringer.

Only take reputable taxis.

Use cards instead of cash.

Shred documents, especially any displaying credit card, bank account, or government ID numbers.

Verify communications from banks, utilities, and commerce sites. Never e-mail passwords or account numbers.

Only provide government ID number when legally required.

Be wary of unsolicited business calls.

Use your credit card only on reputable sites.

Keep sensitive information and documents in a secured space.

Review your credit report annually.

Don't carry sensitive ID materials with you.

Start a neighborhood watch.

Install an alarm system.

Add motion-sensor lights.

Trim trees away from house.

Store ladders and bins inside.

Keep garage doors locked.

Secure sliding windows.

Look before answering door.

check a car before a trip

To have a safe and uneventful road trip, give your car a once-over before you start your journey.

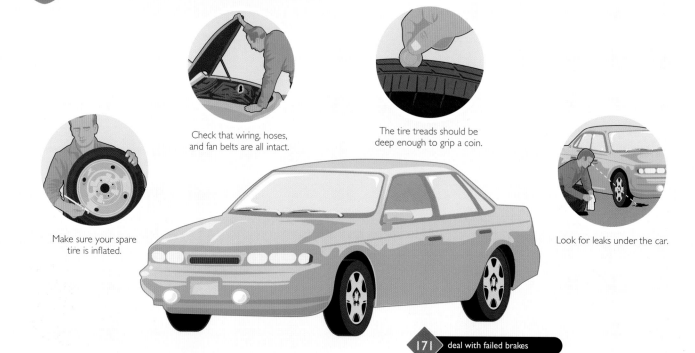

Check that wiring, hoses, and fan belts are all intact.

The tire treads should be deep enough to grip a coin.

Make sure your spare tire is inflated.

Look for leaks under the car.

171 deal with failed brakes

pack a car emergency kit

emergency signals

snow chains and tow chains

jumper cables

warm clothes

multipurpose tool

tools and work gloves

nonperishable foods

bottled water

spare tire and tire-changing tools

tire-repair compound

windshield scraper and cleaner

map and compass

first-aid kit

scissors and cord

candles, matches, flashlight, and batteries

Avoid parking between vans.

Find an open, well-lit area.

Park near an exit.

Use elevator, not stairs.

Have keys out upon return.

Look before getting into car.

Lock the doors immediately.

Leave the garage at once.

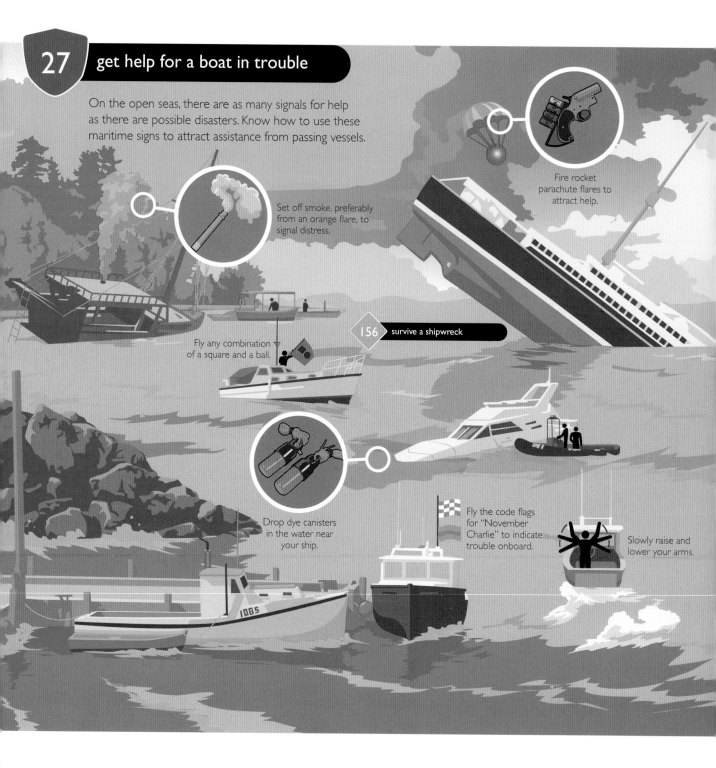

On the open seas, there are as many signals for help as there are possible disasters. Know how to use these maritime signs to attract assistance from passing vessels.

Fire rocket parachute flares to attract help.

Set off smoke, preferably from an orange flare, to signal distress.

Fly any combination of a square and a ball.

156 > survive a shipwreck

Drop dye canisters in the water near your ship.

Fly the code flags for "November Charlie" to indicate trouble onboard.

Slowly raise and lower your arms.

cumulonimbus
Beware this fierce storm cloud, recognizable by its distinctive anvil shape.

stratocumulus
Watch these lumpy rows closely, as a change in air density can turn them into stormy nimbostratus.

cumulus
Keep an eye on these small, lumpy clouds—rising hot air can turn them into a thundering cumulonimbus.

nimbostratus
Bringers of rain, snow, and danger, these ragged-bottomed clouds are an ominous gray.

Take waves at an angle.

Secure loose items.

Close all hatches and portals.

Unplug electrical equipment.

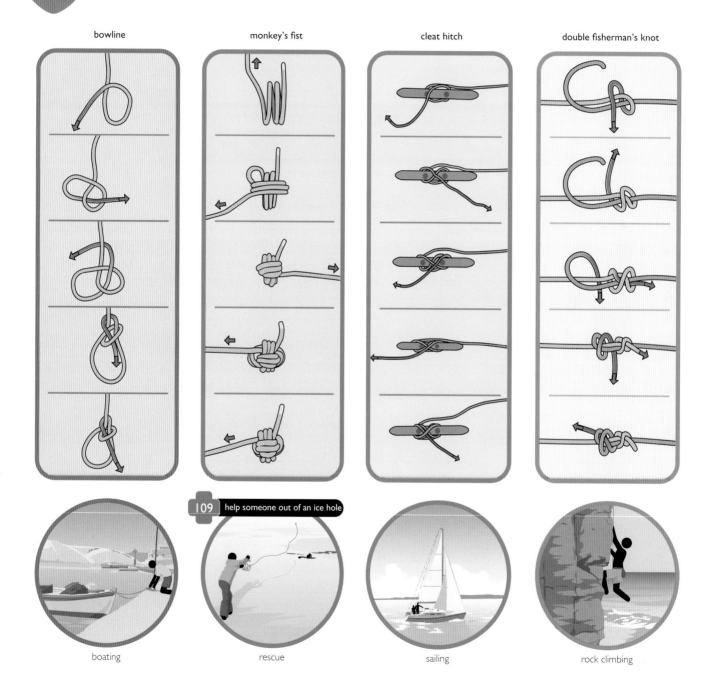

bowline

monkey's fist

cleat hitch

double fisherman's knot

109 help someone out of an ice hole

boating

rescue

sailing

rock climbing

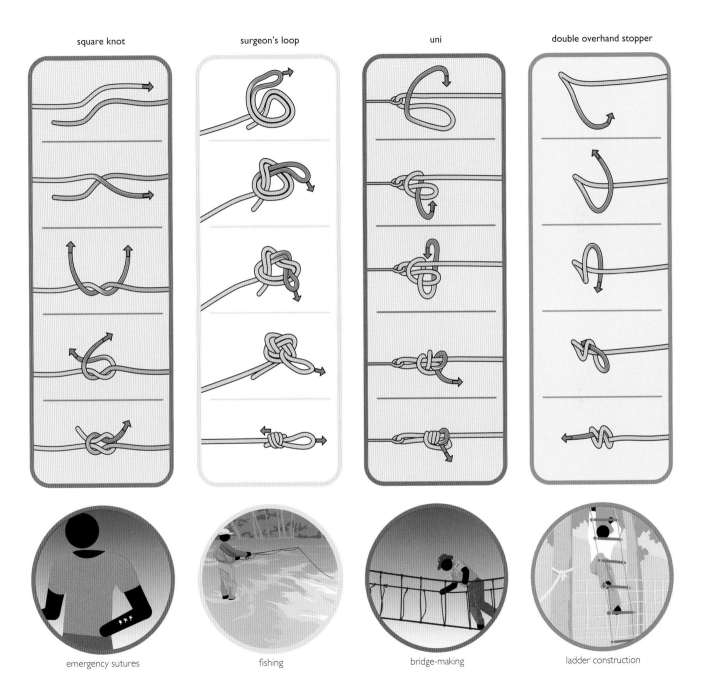

square knot

surgeon's loop

uni

double overhand stopper

emergency sutures

fishing

bridge-making

ladder construction

31 sleep on the beach

Use damp sand to scrub dishes.

Camp well above the line of debris marking high tide.

Don't bring glass bottles.

A tarp lean-to provides shade.

Keep towels and a brush handy at the tent's opening.

Weight tent lines and bury in sand instead of using spikes.

Fully extinguish fires before burying coals.

32 pitch a snow camp

Pack down a flat spot with skis, then pitch tent on top.

Tie tent lines to rocks and bury in the snow.

Don't use camp stove inside tent.

Don't pitch tent in avalanche-prone areas.

Dig a pit at tent opening for putting on and removing boots.

Run melted snow through a coffee filter before drinking.

III save a hypothermia victim

shelter in the jungle

33

Don't feed the wildlife!

Hold a flame to leeches to remove; don't pull.

Sleep on a raised platform with a rain tarp and mosquito netting.

Seal food in plastic containers and store outside of tent.

Leave perfume and deodorant at home.

Camp well away from pesky insect nests.

Shake out sleeping bags before getting in.

Pitch tent at least 25 ft (7.5 m) above any water source.

treat a snake bite 150

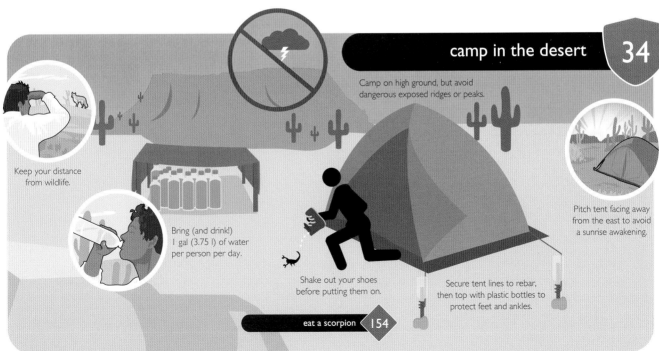

camp in the desert

34

Keep your distance from wildlife.

Bring (and drink!) 1 gal (3.75 l) of water per person per day.

Camp on high ground, but avoid dangerous exposed ridges or peaks.

Shake out your shoes before putting them on.

Secure tent lines to rebar, then top with plastic bottles to protect feet and ankles.

Pitch tent facing away from the east to avoid a sunrise awakening.

eat a scorpion 154

With proper preparation, you and your family can live happy, productive lives as Rome burns around you.

Have ample food stores.

Have solid home defenses in place.

Know your neighbors and your extended community.

Glassblowing will be a useful skill after the collapse.

Learn to can and preserve fresh foods.

Trade and barter supplies and skills with neighbors.

Secure an armory of weapons and ammunition.

Take up rope-making to create a valuable commodity.

Chemists who can produce medicine and fertilizer will be in high demand after a collapse.

Invest in a portable, hand-cranked radio.

Backyard chickens will be worth their weight in gold.

Grow a garden full of hardy, tasty foods.

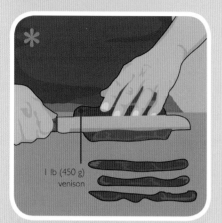

1 lb (450 g) venison

Slice venison into thin strips.

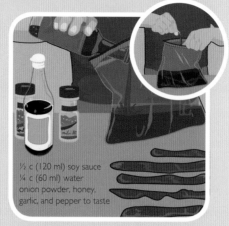

½ c (120 ml) soy sauce
¼ c (60 ml) water
onion powder, honey, garlic, and pepper to taste

Mix marinade in a large plastic bag.

8–12 hrs

Marinate in the refrigerator overnight.

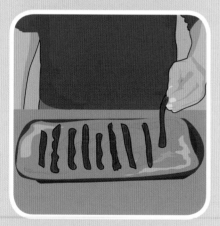

Lay on a parchment-paper–lined pan.

4–8 hrs

200°F (93°C)

Bake until chewy but not crispy.

Take your jerky on the road!

Why limit yourself to just venison? Jerky can be made out of beef, salmon, turkey, and even shark! Vegetarians can use tofu or mushrooms. Play with spices and proteins for a portable, practical food.

Smoking a piece of meat can safely extend its shelf life by several weeks (or longer if it's frozen after smoking) by removing water and killing bacteria. You can make this tasty survivalist food at home by building your own simple smoker.

marinated meat

metal grate

smoke

wood chips

chip box

hot plate

garbage can

cinder blocks

+ + + + +

Should food in your suburb become scarce, it will help to have a dog trained to "tree" small game. Give yourself and your pooch a few weeks to master all the stages of training.

Toss a ball and say "Squirrel 'em!"

Say "Squirrel 'em" and point up.

Release squirrel; allow dog to tree it.

Reward dog for barking.

Train your dog to chase a squirrel pelt on a rope.

Train dog to bark at the caged squirrel in a tree.

Introduce dog to a live, caged squirrel.

Reward dog for barking.

Sling the pelt over a branch; encourage dog to bark at it.

protect a baby bird 103

Scatter birdseed each day.

Scatter seed; stand nearby.

Stand nearby, holding a box.

Drop box on tasty pigeons.

feed a family without a farm 40

A patch of dirt and a detailed plan is all you need to achieve vegetable self-sufficiency.

Divide plot into 12-in-by-12-in (30-cm-by-30-cm) squares.

Choose vegetable varieties that grow vertically to increase the square's yield.

Plant tall plants at plot's edge to keep their shadows off adjacent plants.

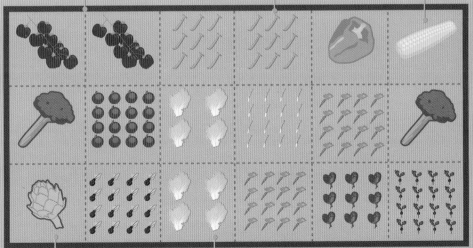

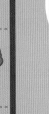

Replant as soon as you harvest.

Variety is the spice of life! Plant and enjoy a wide range of nutritious crops year-round.

Put shallow-rooted plants next to deep-rooted ones so they don't compete for resources.

eat wild around the world 155

Fertilize soil year-round.

The outdoors can be physically grueling. Keep your body in top shape so you can conquer whatever nature throws your way.

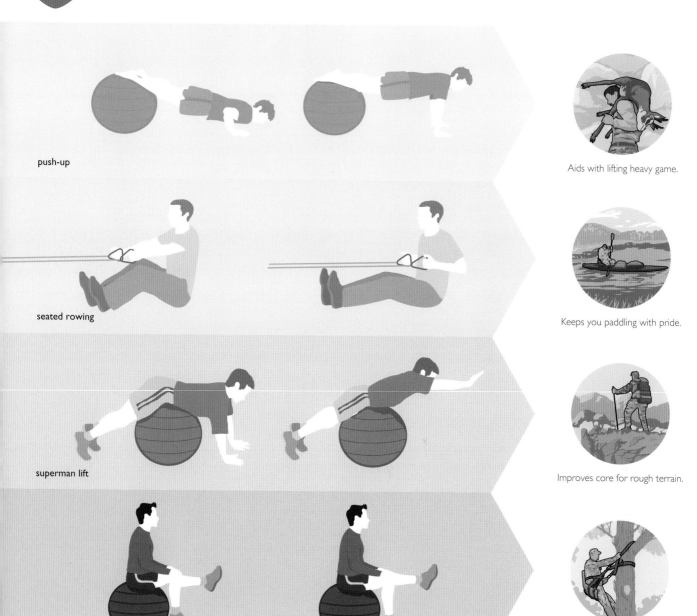

push-up

Aids with lifting heavy game.

seated rowing

Keeps you paddling with pride.

superman lift

Improves core for rough terrain.

seated leg lift

Assists in tree-climbing skills.

chair dip

Builds body for dragging trophy.

supine lift

Helps with hauling gear.

scissors

Supports cliff climbing.

ball squats

Enhances uphill hiking endurance.

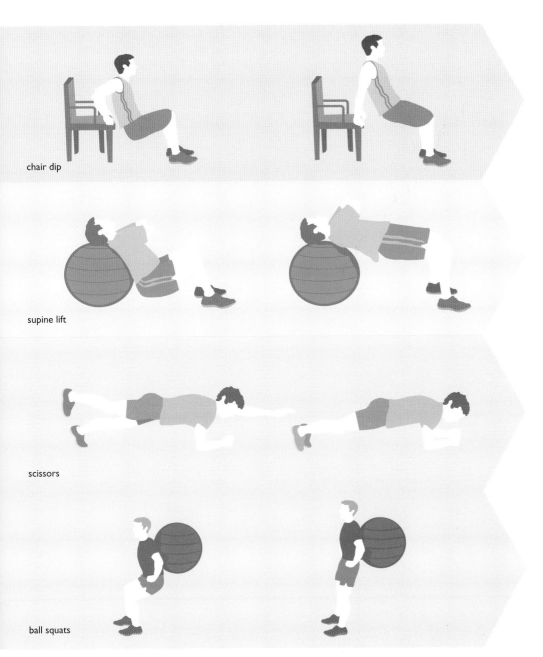

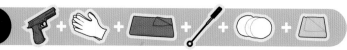

Verify gun is unloaded.

Disassemble gun.

Clean the bore of the barrel.

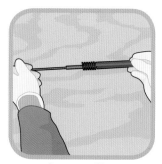
Remove residue.

Run cloths down the barrel.

Clean the slide.

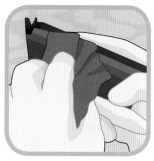
Clean the magazine.

Reassemble; wipe off excess.

43 store a gun

Unload before storing.

Use a cable lock.

Store guns and ammo apart.

Secure the key to the safe.

Use a case or a holster.

Verify the range is clear.

Load the gun.

Keep finger off trigger.

Always point downrange.

Enter stance; turn off safety.

Line up your sight.

Squeeze the trigger.

disarm a shooter **45**

Sidestep and grab the wrist.

Twist to break finger.

Grip and pull down.

Take control.

Wash your hands frequently.

Avoid touching door handles.

Keep your distance from strangers.

If you feel sick, stay home.

Cover mouth when coughing or sneezing.

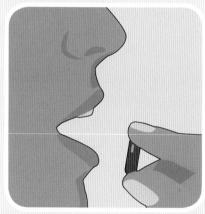

Take antiviral medication if prescribed.

disposable nonlatex gloves

aloe vera gel

antihistamine lotion

calamine lotion

hydrogen peroxide

rubbing alcohol

hydrocortisone cream

bandage shears

assorted adhesive bandages

sunscreen

burn gel

triangular bandage

splint

tweezers

thermometer

irrigation syringe

suction bulb

safety pins

cotton swabs

gauze roller bandages

adhesive roller bandages

trauma shears

breathing barrier

burn dressing

absorbent compress dressings

antibiotic ointment

assorted gauze pads

cold compress

mild soap

adhesive cloth tape

cotton balls

ibuprofen

aspirin

activated charcoal

first-aid manual

emergency contacts

antiseptic wipes

eye cups

eyewash

antihistamines

syrup of ipecac

extra prescription medications

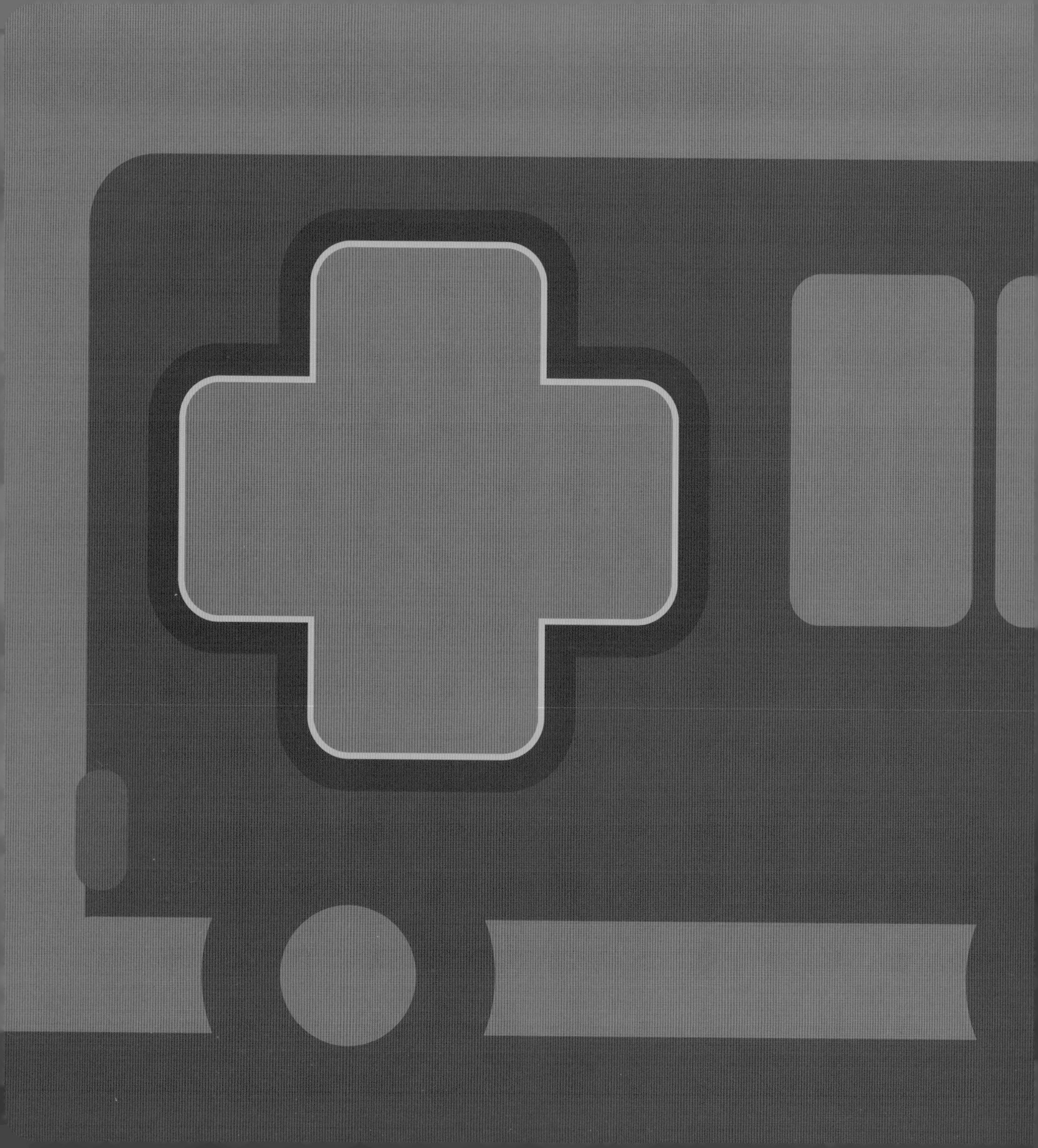

Oh, man! A jellyfish just stung your buddy, there's a fishhook stuck in your finger, and your hunting cabin has burst into flames. Worst vacation ever? Not if you know what to do (and no, it doesn't involve peeing on anyone. Sorry!). When things start going wrong, you can totally be the hero who has studied up on what to do and is ready, willing, and able to help out. Studies show that people who have thought about possible scenarios and planned out what they'd do are the ones who stay calm when things start falling apart around them. So read up, and be sure you really know how to handle tough situations. You (and your friend with the jellyfish sting) will be glad you did.

help

help after an accident

Assess the situation.

Elevate the victim's legs.

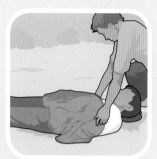

Keep him warm.

Help is on the way.

Reassure the victim.

call for help

Observe accident details.

Call within view of accident.

Stay calm; answer questions.

Gather info to recount later.

| Find the Adam's apple. | Move to side, under jaw. | Press gently with two fingers. | Count beats. |

 Multiply by four to get the beats per minute. Generally, a pulse below sixty bpm or above one hundred is cause for concern.

| Treat any minor injuries. | Call back if situation changes. | Stay until responders arrive. | Provide information. |

51   bolt from a wrist grip

 The weak spot is in between the first two fingers, right below the knuckles.

Make a fist with free hand.

Aim for his hand's weak spot.

Hit point with your knuckle.

Once free, run.

Punching with your thumb inside your fingers can lead to a fight-ending broken thumb.

Hold your fist loosely and strike with the knuckles of your first two fingers.

52   escape from a choke hold

Raise your elbow; turn.

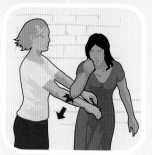

Break hold with your elbow.

Join your hands.

Push your elbow to strike.

A quick strike on these weak spots can disable an attacker long enough for you to escape to safety.

eyes
Poke, scratch, or spit at to disorient.

ears
Slap or pull to stun.

nose
Strike to cause whiplash or bleeding.

adam's apple
Hit to knock the wind out of attacker.

underarm
Punch to disable arm.

groin
Kick, knee, strike, or squeeze to immobilize a male attacker.

kneecap
Stomp or knock sideways to disable legs.

instep and toes
Stomp to stun or knock attacker off balance.

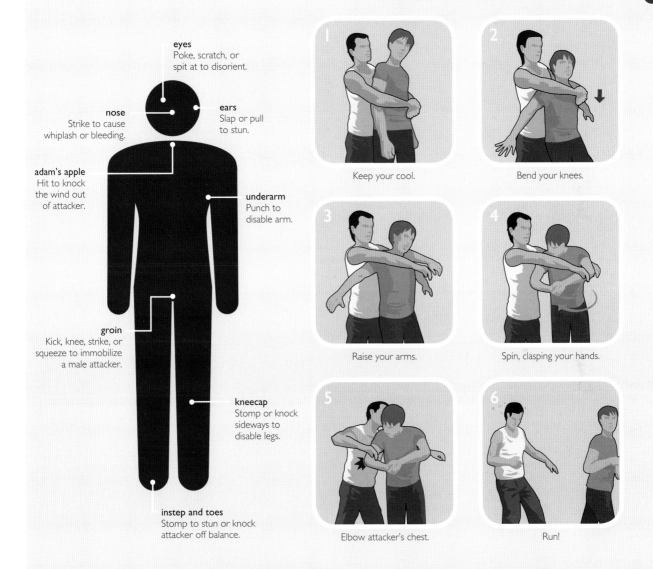

1. Keep your cool.

2. Bend your knees.

3. Raise your arms.

4. Spin, clasping your hands.

5. Elbow attacker's chest.

6. Run!

54 deal with a burgled home

Stay calm.

Call the police.

Assume intruder is there.

Wait for help with a friend.

55 follow up after a burglary

Contact your insurance.

Change your locks.

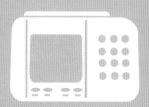

Consider an alarm system.

Inform your neighbors.

Only enter with the police.

Avoid contaminating scene.

Check all closets thoroughly.

Only clean when authorized.

Write a list of missing items.

Inventory your prescriptions.

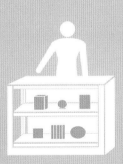

Check out local pawn shops.

Inspect online marketplaces.

perform cpr on an adult

Tilt head back; lift the chin.

Listen for breathing.

Briefly feel for a pulse.

Visually confirm airway is clear.

Pinch and hold the nostrils.

Breathe for the victim.

Pump on the breastbone.

Repeat until help arrives.

do the heimlich maneuver

Are you choking?

Assess the situation.

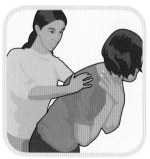

Stand behind the victim.

Place your fist below her ribs.

Cover your fist; thrust inward.

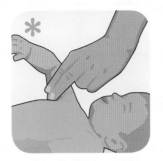

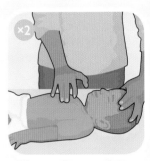

Check breath without tilting head.

Check pulse.

Give small rescue puffs.

Press quickly with two fingers.

 The best place to feel a baby's pulse is in the brachial artery. Using two fingers (not a thumb), press around the area inside the arm, above the elbow crease, until you locate a pulse.

 Smoothly thrust straight down on the chest ½ to 1 in (1.25–2.5 cm), then allow the chest to come back to its normal position.

Listen for breathing.

Strike the baby's back.

Thrust on sternum.

Check for breathing; repeat.

60 improvise an airway puncture

Extend neck; find spot for incision.

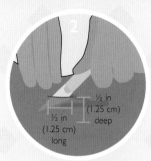

½ in (1.25 cm) deep
½ in (1.25 cm) long

Hold skin taut; make incision through the skin.

Puncture membrane; enlarge hole with a finger.

Insert an empty pen barrel into the hole.

This procedure, known as a cricothyrotomy or emergency airway puncture, is an absolute last resort in a situation where a victim's airway is blocked.

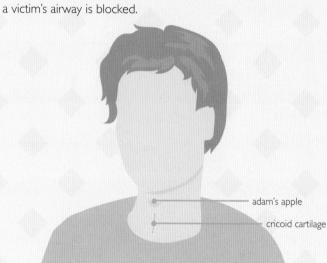

adam's apple

cricoid cartilage

Feel for the soft spot between the Adam's apple and the cricoid cartilage. Keep your finger there to guide the knife.

61 suture a wound

Clean wound.

Align edges of wound.

¹⁄₁₀–⁴⁄₁₀ in (0.1–0.3 cm)

Stitch; tighten suture.

30 know your knots

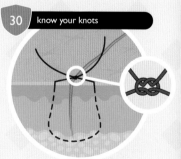

Secure with a square knot. Repeat to seal wound.

A tension pneumothorax occurs when air or gas fills the chest cavity, preventing a lung from expanding.

This emergency chest decompression method is high on the list of things you should never do.

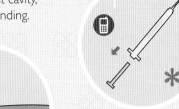

Remove stopper from syringe.

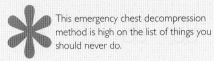

Apply airtight bandage over the wound.

Sterilize the needle.

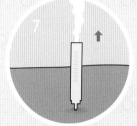

normal lung and cavity

insertion site

air-filled cavity

deflated lung

insertion site

midclavicular line

third rib

second rib

Locate the insertion site.

Listen for a hiss from the needle; let air escape.

Feel for the pop.

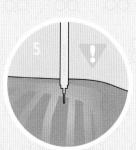

Insert at right angle.

Clean insertion site.

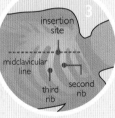

63   stop bleeding

Elevate; apply pressure.

Remove any constrictions.

Layer gauze as needed.

Tape gauze in place.

64   bandage a nasty wound

Elevate and wash site.

Assess need for stitches.

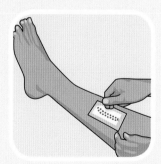

Add non-adhering bandage.

Cover with gauze.

If the wound is so deep that you see yellow fatty tissue, or if it's hard to pinch closed, it needs stitches.

cauterize a wound in the field 65

Heat knife to red hot.

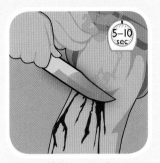

Hold to wound.

Remove; repeat.

Bandage wound.

✳ This neat trick is both risky and incredibly painful. Only try this in the case of a massively bleeding wound when help is days away.

save a toe 66

Pick up the toe.

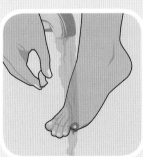

Wash wound and toe.

Add butterfly strips, gauze.

treat frostbite 110

Fully insulate toe; put on ice.

✳ If there are skin flaps left, fold them over the wound before bandaging. Don't put adhesive directly onto an open wound.

67 improvise a leg splint

Avoid moving injured limb.

Treat any open wounds.

Fold cardboard in thirds.

Add padding.

Position extra padding.

Slip under limb.

Secure the splint.

Check for sensation.

68 wrap a sling

Drape fabric under arm.

Draw end over shoulder.

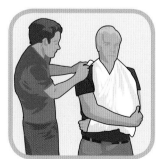
Tie behind neck.

Secure to stabilize.

Bone fractures are as unique and terrible as the accidents that cause them. Here are the most common fractures.

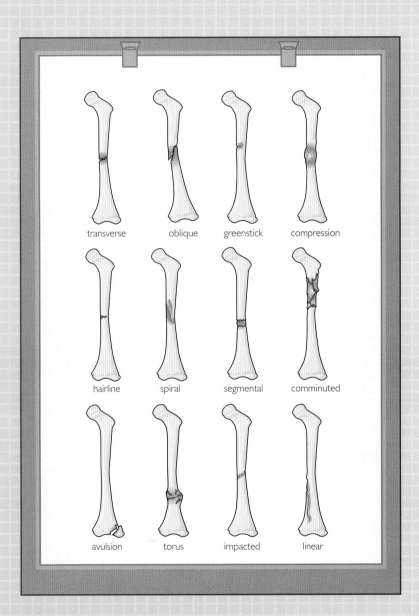

transverse   oblique   greenstick   compression

hairline   spiral   segmental   comminuted

avulsion   torus   impacted   linear

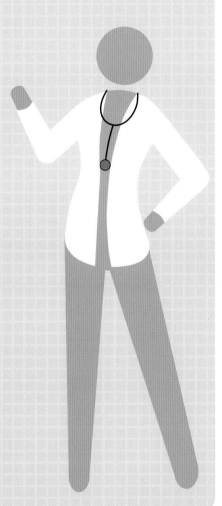

Divide plant parts; test each.

Check for foul odors.

Rub; monitor your reaction.

Rub on your lips.

Touch to your tongue.

Chew; hold in your mouth.

Swallow; wait and monitor.

Bon appétit!

The key to testing for edibility is time. Execute each step with plenty of time in between. Make sure you don't have reactions to possible toxins or allergins. Don't take any unnecessary chances.

Call poison control.

Monitor victim's breathing.

Give ipecac if directed.

Reserve sample of vomit.

 Know your national poison control hotline number. Call at the first sign of trouble and be prepared to stay on the line until directed to hang up. Know your household poisons and keep them in a childproofed place.

cleaning supplies

paint

batteries

insecticide

medicine

elderberry roots

tomato leaves and stems

green potatoes

rhubarb leaves

philodendron

amanita muscaria mushroom

raw almonds

castor beans

identify venomous insects

Nature is nothing to mess with—danger can come in many forms. Here are some examples of venemous insects to avoid. A bite would certainly be enough to ruin your day, and in some cases, could be lethal.

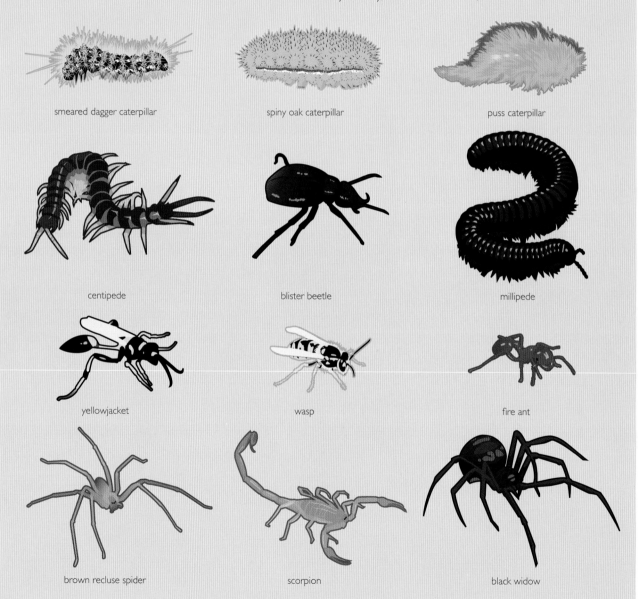

smeared dagger caterpillar

spiny oak caterpillar

puss caterpillar

centipede

blister beetle

millipede

yellowjacket

wasp

fire ant

brown recluse spider

scorpion

black widow

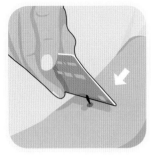

Quickly remove the stinger.

Clean with rubbing alcohol.

Apply baking soda and water.

Apply ice.

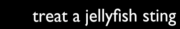

Treating a jellyfish sting with urine is an urban myth. As funny as it might be to pee on your friend's wound, it could make things worse.

Rinse with salt water.

Scrape away tentacles.

Take pain reliever.

Submerge in warm water.

Cut gauze to fit chest.

Mix into a paste.

Microwave.

Spread paste on gauze.

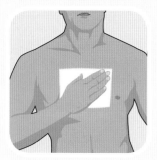

Apply paste side to chest.

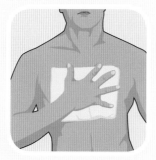

Add a warm compress.

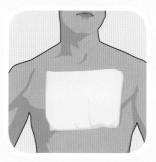

Leave for thirty minutes.

Rinse off with a warm cloth.

Ginger is a wonder food and is good for almost everything that ails you. Make a poultice to ease chest congestions. You can also drink, chew, eat or swallow your way to better health.

tea
Helps with colds.

candy
Relieves pain.

pills
Aids motion sickness.

raw
Eases digestion.

Need a pill in a pinch? Some medicines are safe to use years after their expiration dates. Others quickly become useless, or even dangerous. If it's a lifesaving medicine, or it looks or smells wrong, don't take a chance!

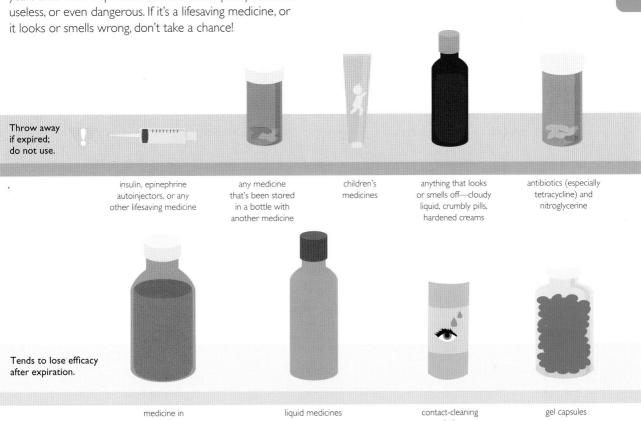

Throw away if expired; do not use.

insulin, epinephrine autoinjectors, or any other lifesaving medicine

any medicine that's been stored in a bottle with another medicine

children's medicines

anything that looks or smells off—cloudy liquid, crumbly pills, hardened creams

antibiotics (especially tetracycline) and nitroglycerine

Tends to lose efficacy after expiration.

medicine in suspension

liquid medicines

contact-cleaning solution

gel capsules

Safe to use up to ten years after expiration.

indigestion or heartburn pills

pain relievers

over-the-counter allergy medicines

headache pills

cold and flu pills

78 remove a small fish hook

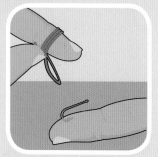
Wrap a string around finger.

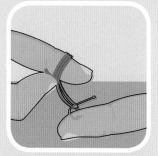
Loop string in bend of hook.

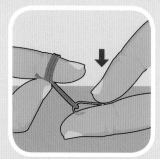
Push down to free barb.

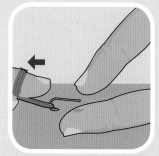
Pull string to pop out hook.

80 remove a splinter

Wash site; sanitize tools.

Squeeze around the splinter.

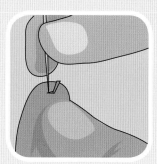
Enlarge the hole with a pin.

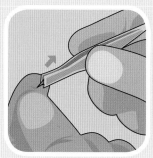
Remove with tweezers.

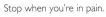 

Stop when you're in pain.

Cut moleskin.

Place moleskin on foot.

Put on a fresh dry sock.

Wash your hands first.

Swab; remove the object.

Lie down; flush with saline.

Turn head to drain excess.

put out a clothing fire

Stay calm.

Lay victim on ground.

Sweep from head to toe.

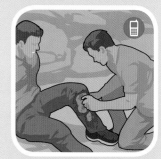

Treat burns.

If you're on fire and no one is around to help, it's time to stop, drop, and roll. Here's how.

stop
Don't run or flail.

drop
Get down on the ground.

roll
Roll to smother flames.

halt an electrocution

Avoid conductors like water.

Get a nonconductive object.

Strike to break current.

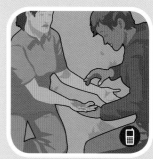

Assess burns.

Separate yourself from other people.

Remove metal and jewelry from body.

Put down an insulating layer if possible.

Walk down to a lower position; avoid trees.

Crouch with hands off ground and mouth open.

identify burns

Second-degree burns are so last century. Nowadays, in-the-know burn victims classify their wounds by the depth of epidermal damage.

 19 be prepared in a house fire

full-thickness burn

partial-thickness burn

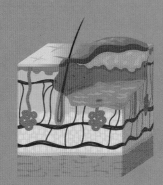

superficial burn

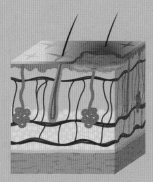

blisters, patchy white or red areas with black edges, may or may not be painful

blisters, red weeping skin, quite painful

redness, dry skin, pain

 +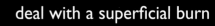

Soothe with a cold cloth.

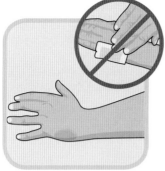

Keep it exposed to air.

Take pain reliever.

Monitor for discoloration.

 +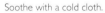

Stay calm.

Brush off dry chemicals.

Flush out remaining bits.

Pat dry.

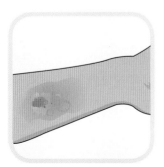

Leave embedded material.

Put antibiotic on open sores.

Cover with sterile gauze.

Seek medical attention.

Remove anything near neck.

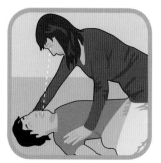
Check that airway is clear.

Put soft object under head.

Remove hazards from area.

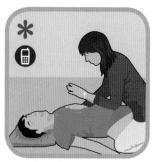
Note duration of attack.

Keep bystanders away.

Place in recovery position.

Explain what happened.

If a person is unconscious or semiconscious, place him in the recovery position to keep him breathing safely. Here's how.

* If the seizure lasts for more than five minutes, call an ambulance.

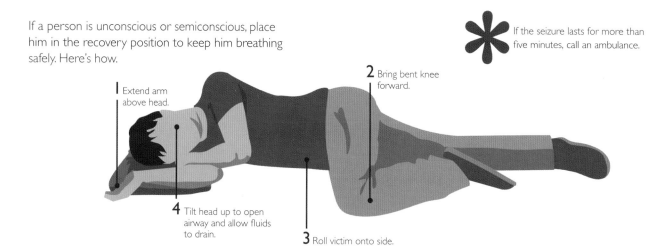

1 Extend arm above head.

2 Bring bent knee forward.

4 Tilt head up to open airway and allow fluids to drain.

3 Roll victim onto side.

pressure, squeezing, or
pain in center of chest

tightness, burning, or pain
in arms, neck, jaw, or back

faint, increased,
or irregular pulse

cold sweat, dizziness,
pallor, anxiety, or fear

 A heart attack victim may experience any of these symptoms in varying degrees of intensity, and the symptoms may abate and then reappear. If you suspect a heart attack, call for an ambulance immediately.

 If you notice any of these symptoms take immediate action, even if the symptoms appear to go away. Early intervention during a stroke can reduce long-term disability.

weakness, facial droop, or
tingling on one or both sides
of body

confusion; trouble speaking
or understanding

sudden, severe headache;
trouble seeing

dizziness; loss of balance

153 prepare tasty snake meat

Remove source of anxiety.

Slow down.

Encourage slower breathing.

Raise victim's head.

×10

Have him breathe into bag.

Stay calm.

Use inhaler if available.

Have someone sit with you.

Inhale through nose.

Purse lips; exhale slowly.

Get away from triggers.

10 min

Seek aid if attack lasts.

Discuss asthma care plan.

 + + +

Calm and reassure victim.

Identify and isolate allergen.

calamine lotion

If rash appears, apply lotion.

Apply a cold compress.

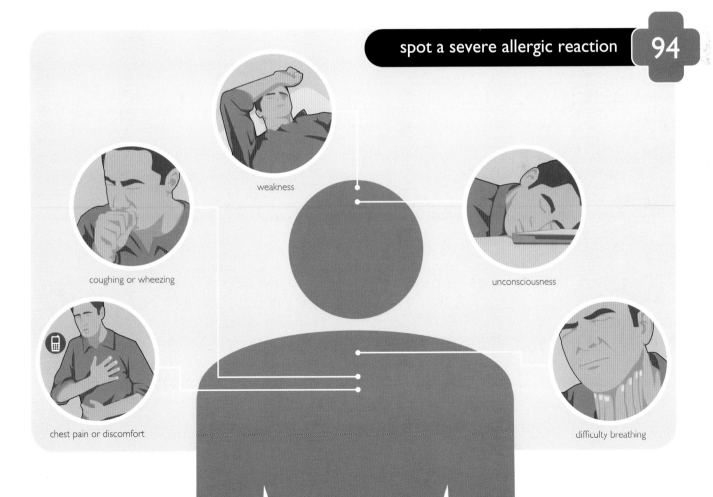

weakness

coughing or wheezing

unconsciousness

chest pain or discomfort

difficulty breathing

Apply intermittent pressure.

Lean forward.

Catch blood with a cloth.

If bleeding persists, get help.

Different nosebleeds may respond to different approaches. Here are some alternate abatement methods to try.

Try pushing on your upper lip.

If it's caused by dryness, breathe into a damp cloth.

Keep victim still and calm.

Pour warm water.

Gently ease tongue away.

Comfort victim.

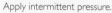

Hold by crown, not roots.

Clean in bowl of warm water.

Place in glass of milk.

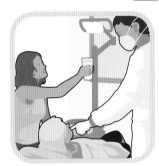

Bring to a dentist.

Wash hands thoroughly.

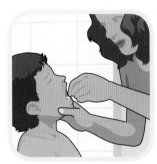

Remove pieces of tooth.

Rinse with disinfected water.

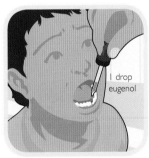

I drop eugenol

Apply to reduce pain.

Roll melted wax into a ball.

Place wax filling in gap.

Bite to set in place.

See a dentist.

Check for spinal cord injury.

Put cold compress on bump.

Keep victim still.

Wake; assess condition.

nausea, vomiting

inappropriate outbursts

short-term memory loss, confusion

uneven pupils

blurred or double vision, light sensitivity, seeing spots

headaches, sleepiness, unconsciousness

mood swings, personality changes

unusual irritability

 If you suspect a skull fracture, do not apply pressure. Call for medical aid immediately. The victim can take a pain medication that doesn't contain aspirin.

No matter how upset the kid is, don't pick her up or put your arms around her—a pat on the arm will be enough. Stay with her where you found her.

Crouch to child's eye level.

Ask if she's lost her parents.

Comfort her without holding or picking up.

Reassure her.

Ask for parents' details.

Stay put and await help—don't walk off.

Call police or store security.

Stay with child until help arrives.

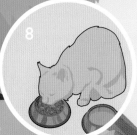

Feed cat immediately.

Locate stranded cat.

Cut a slit in the side
of a pillowcase.

Cinch top; climb down.

Stitch a work glove
to slit in pillowcase.

Pull bag inside out,
enclosing cat.

Grab cat by the
scruff of the neck.

Climb tree; don glove.

Pull tongue forward.

Close mouth.

Cover snout and breathe.

Repeat every three seconds.

 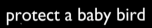
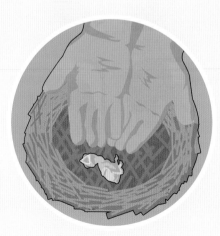

If bird is featherless,
replace in nest.

Call a wildlife aid center.

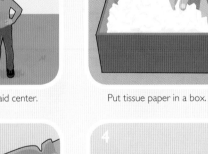

Put tissue paper in a box.

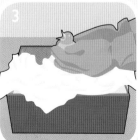

Place bird in box.

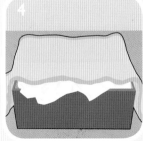

Cover loosely with a towel.

1 Grab a towel or jacket.

162 ace an emergency scuba ascent

2 Swim out to the victim.

Stop short; throw the towel.

Let victim get a grip.

A panicked swimmer may try to climb on top of you. For your safety and hers, keep your distance and use a rescue aid, like a towel or rope.

Swim in, pulling victim.

Get medical aid if needed.

Heat exhaustion is an easily treatable illness brought on by exposure to—you guessed it—heat. If ignored, it can progress into life-threatening heat stroke, which requires emergency care. Here's how to tell the difference.

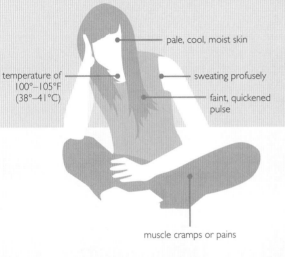

pale, cool, moist skin

temperature of 100°–105°F (38°–41°C)

sweating profusely

faint, quickened pulse

muscle cramps or pains

heat exhaustion

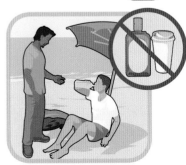

unconscious or unusual mental state

temperature over 105°F (41°C)

rapid pulse

flushed, hot, dry skin

heat stroke

Check victim's temperature.

Shade him; remove clothes.

Bathe with cool water.

Give him plenty to drink.

help clean up an oil spill

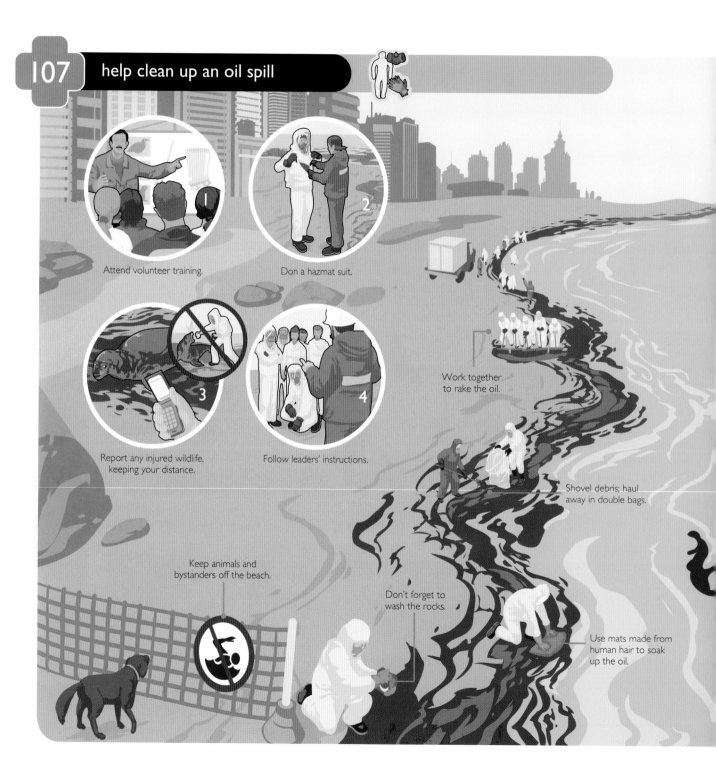

Attend volunteer training.

Don a hazmat suit.

Report any injured wildlife, keeping your distance.

Follow leaders' instructions.

Work together to rake the oil.

Shovel debris; haul away in double bags.

Keep animals and bystanders off the beach.

Don't forget to wash the rocks.

Use mats made from human hair to soak up the oil.

Pilot a boom boat to the edge of the spill.

Contain the slick with the oil boom.

Safely capture the bird.

Clean mucous membranes.

99 parts clean water
1 part dishwashing liquid

Wash; repeat until clean.

Gently dry with warm air.

Place in warm water.

Release.

Get training before trying to clean oiled wildlife.

Anchor yourself.

Crawl out with a stick.

Let victim take hold.

Pull while victim kicks out.

save a hypothermia victim

95°F
(35°C)

Assess body temperature.

Monitor shivering.

133 dig a snow cave

Remove from exposure.

Handle the victim gently.

 Other signs of hypothermia include sluggishness, disorientation, and general fatigue. If a person suddenly stops violently shivering, the case is severe and you should get help as soon as possible.

Look for waxy or white skin.

Remove constricting items.

Soak in warm water.

Separate the digits; wrap.

Remove any wet clothing.

Insulate the victim.

Serve a hot beverage.

Share heat.

When things get crazy, and that fight-or-flight instinct kicks in, it's natural to get a kind of tunnel vision and stop thinking rationally. You need to combat this habit, or else not only will you fail to rescue anyone, you'll end up needing to be rescued yourself. And that's just embarrassing. The real survival rock star has spent some time thinking about how they'd handle getting lost in the woods, attacked by pit bulls, bitten by poisonous snakes, and shipwrecked at sea . . . although hopefully not all at once. If it happened though, and you'd memorized everything in this book, you would totally prevail. Just stay calm, remember to protect yourself, communicate well with others, focus on teamwork . . . and most importantly, show that man-eating shark who's boss. You rock!

prevail

If you want others to be able to follow your path in the wild, make these international trailblazing symbols using grass, sticks, or rocks.

not the way

turn left

danger

tubelike with
tapered ends

teardrop shaped

pellets with
bone and hair

birds of prey

cat family

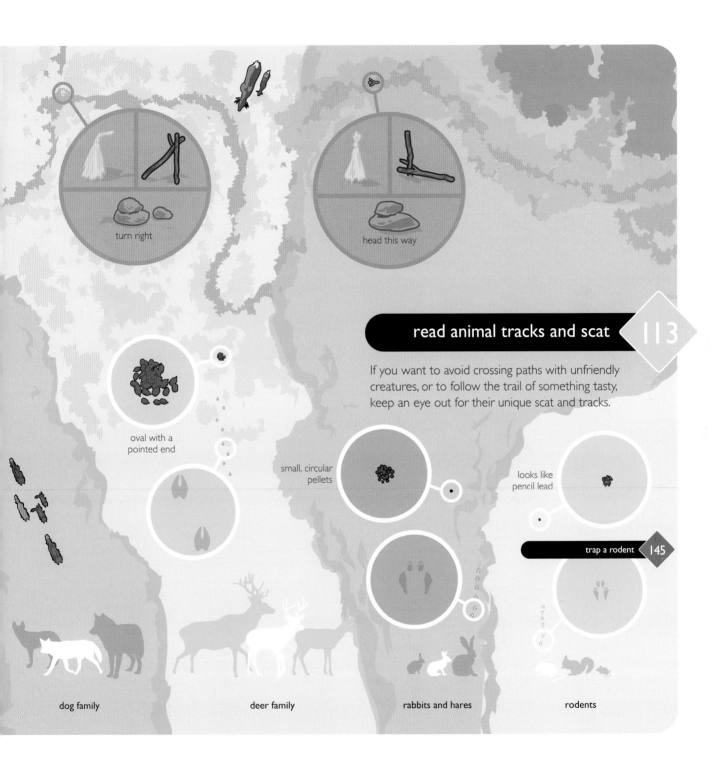

turn right

head this way

If you want to avoid crossing paths with unfriendly creatures, or to follow the trail of something tasty, keep an eye out for their unique scat and tracks.

oval with a
pointed end

small, circular
pellets

looks like
pencil lead

trap a rodent 145

dog family

deer family

rabbits and hares

rodents

walk a straight line in the woods

Most of the time, you're probably pretty good at walking in a straight line. In the wilderness, it's almost impossible due to uneven terrain and obstacles. Use this trick to stay on track.

Choose your direction.

Find a landmark in that path.

Walk toward the landmark.

Arrive; pick a new landmark.

navigate with your watch

No compass? No problem! A trusty wristwatch can point you in the right direction.

Northern Hemisphere temperate zones

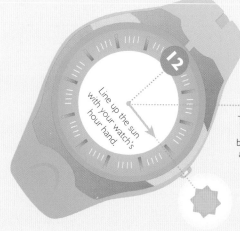

Line up the sun with your watch's hour hand.

N
To find north, imagine a line bisecting the space between the twelve o'clock position and the hour hand.

S
To find south, mentally draw a bisecting line between the hour hand and the twelve o'clock position.

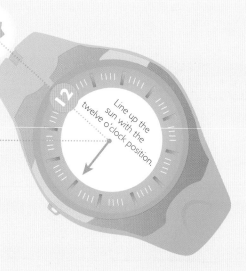

Line up the sun with the twelve o'clock position.

Southern Hemisphere temperate zones

stay on track in the desert

116

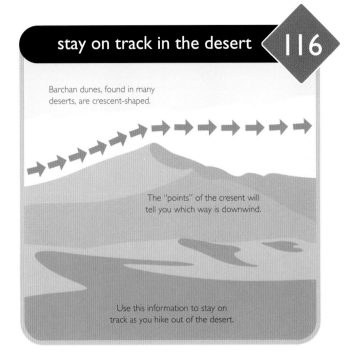

Barchan dunes, found in many deserts, are crescent-shaped.

The "points" of the cresent will tell you which way is downwind.

Use this information to stay on track as you hike out of the desert.

navigate out of a swamp

117

Tie a leaf to a stick and poke the stick into the swamp floor.

Very slowly, the leaf will drift downriver. Head in that direction to reach the ocean (and hopefully other people).

read the stars

118

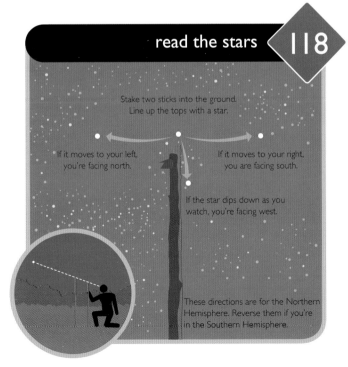

Stake two sticks into the ground. Line up the tops with a star.

If it moves to your left, you're facing north.

If it moves to your right, you are facing south.

If the star dips down as you watch, you're facing west.

These directions are for the Northern Hemisphere. Reverse them if you're in the Southern Hemisphere.

find the equator in a forest

119

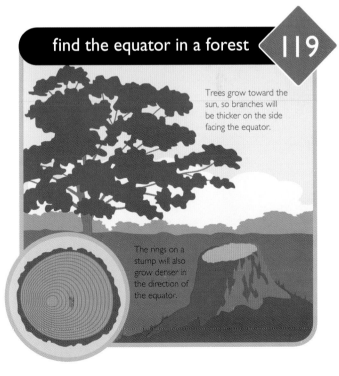

Trees grow toward the sun, so branches will be thicker on the side facing the equator.

The rings on a stump will also grow denser in the direction of the equator.

Make a pile of dry tinder.

Form a teepee of sticks.

Surround with branches.

Ignite tinder.

Unwrap a chocolate bar.

Rub onto soda can bottom.

Focus sunlight onto tinder.

Use tinder to light fire.

Cut a notch in a plank.

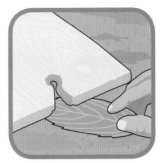

Set a leaf under the notch.

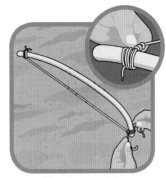

Tie string to a stick.

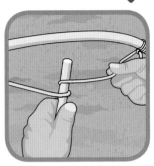

Wrap second stick in string.

Use a rock to hold in place.

Use a sawing motion.

Gather coals; add to tinder.

Blow on tinder to ignite.

use a fire plank 123

Set a leaf beneath a plank.

Gouge a channel into plank.

Dig faster to create coals.

Pour coals onto tinder.

124 · purify water in green bamboo

Cut a stalk of bamboo.

Cut a section to form a cup.

Fill with water.

Bring to a boil; remove cup.

If you need to purify water in the field, use hollow green plants like bamboo or young coconut. The water will boil before the plant burns through.

125 · boil water in a tree stump

Put stones in a campfire.

Pour into hollow stump.

Add hot stones to water.

Continue until boiling.

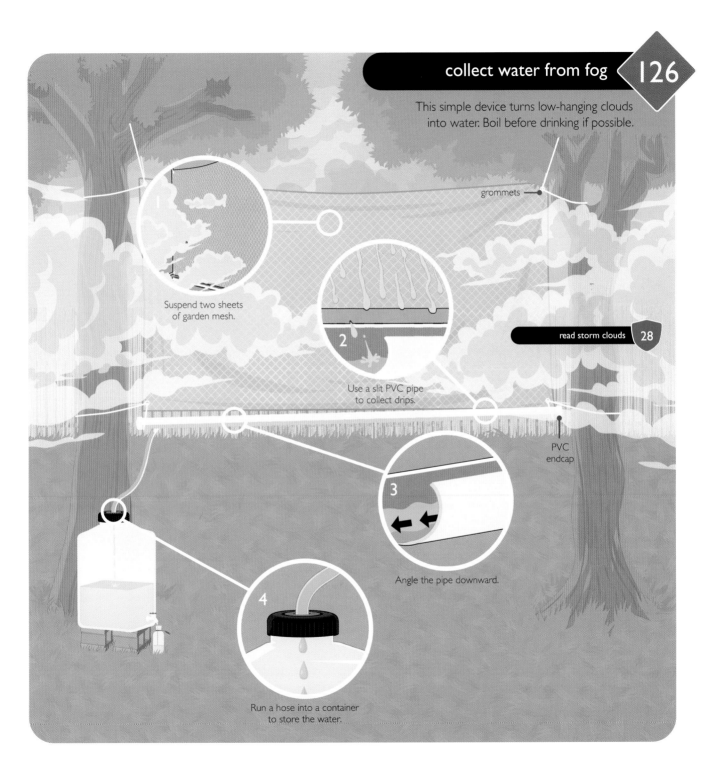

This simple device turns low-hanging clouds into water. Boil before drinking if possible.

grommets

Suspend two sheets of garden mesh.

Use a slit PVC pipe to collect drips.

read storm clouds 28

PVC endcap

Angle the pipe downward.

Run a hose into a container to store the water.

Any waterproof container will do.

The tubing should be at least 3 ft (1 m) in length.

The plastic tarp must be clear.

Medium-sized rocks work best.

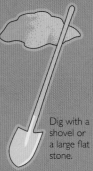

Dig with a shovel or a large flat stone.

Dig deep enough to reach the damper subsoil. You can help the process by by urinating near—but not inside!—the container.

Dig a hole in the sand.

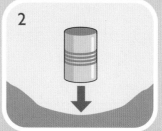

Add a container to collect water.

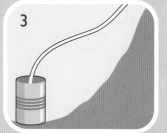

Insert the tubing.

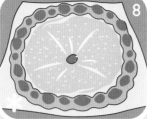

Wait for water to condense.

During daylight hours, water vapor will condense beneath the tarp and drip from its lowest point.

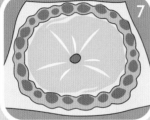

Put a rock in the center.

Yes!
Need help!

No.
Don't need help.

Make symbols on the ground large enough to be seen from above.

I
serious injury

LL
all is well

O
need compass and map

△
believe safe to land here

K
indicate direction to proceed

↑
am going this way

F
need food and water

Seal the airholes with sand.

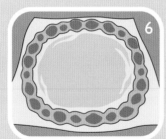

Cover the hole with the tarp.

Anchor the tarp with rocks.

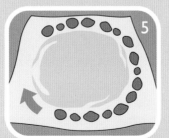

Make symbols using branches, footprints, or any other available material.

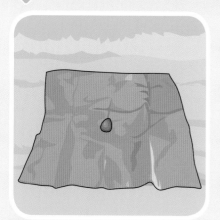

Open a tarp; place rock in the center.

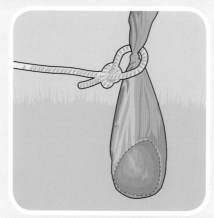

Knot a rope to secure the rock.

Sling the rope over a branch.

Raise the tarp; tie the rope to the trunk.

Spread out the base; secure with rocks.

Add leaves for insulation; climb in!

assemble a debris hut `130`

1 Find a tree with a low crook.

2 Use a sturdy branch as a beam.

3 Add smaller sticks.

4 Roof with leafy branches.

5 Insulate the floor with grass, leaves, or pine needles.

set up a shade shelter `131`

1 Find a natural dip in the land.

2 Dig a space for your body.

3 Stretch a blanket over the hole.

4 Anchor with rocks.

identify heat-related illnesses `105`

build a swamp bed `132`

1 Find four well-spaced trees, or drive bamboo poles into the mud.

2 Measure and cut branches.

3 Make a frame with the long branches; secure with vines.

4 Tie the shorter branches to the frame.

5 Pad with large leaves.

dig a snow cave `133`

treat frostbite `110`

1 Dig into a deep, firm snowdrift.

2 Carve a high sleeping platform.

3 Chisel a floor to trap sinking cold air.

4 Poke a hole for oxygen flow.

5 Seal the entrance with a snowball.

Jump above the break line.

Move perpendicular to flow.

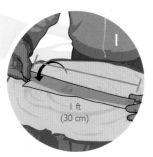

Cut a strip of duct tape; fold.

1 ft
(30 cm)

Make a long slit.

Grab a sturdy tree or rock.

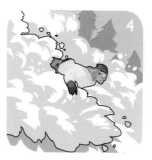

"Swim" on top of snow.

Fasten around head with tape.

Blacken cheeks with soot.

If submerged, cover face.

Make airhole as snow slows.

Snow debris and broken trees
indicate previous avalanches—be
wary of repeat slides.

Avoid avalanche-prone areas in the 48 hours after rough weather or a thaw. If you must go, pack a collapsible shovel, a snow probe, and an avalanche beacon.

Slopes of 30 to 45 degrees are most likely to avalanche, but even slopes of 25 to 60 degrees can slide in certain conditions.

A heavy, compacted layer of snow resting on a powdery layer is highly unstable.

Smooth, grassy slopes without rocks or trees are most dangerous.

Everyone in your party should carry an avalanche beacon. Should you lose someone in an avalanche, you can use your beacon to hone in on the radio signal emitted by the victim's beacon and find them quickly.

Go to location of last sighting.

Set beacon to receive mode.

Poke with snow probe.

Dig downhill from victim.

Uncover head first.

save a hypothermia victim 111

Send for help.

Cut two bottles.

Fit together.

Perforate; stitch together.

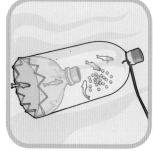

Bait; anchor and submerge.

4 in
(10 cm)

Chisel a hole in thick ice.

Tie line and hook to a forked branch.

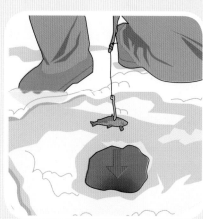

Bait the hook; lower into hole.

Submerge your arm.

Wiggle your fingers.

Scoop up fish.

Fling to shore.

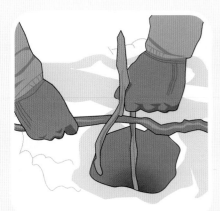

Prop the forked branch with a stick.

Pack to prevent hole from freezing over.

Wait for a bite.

141 **snare a hare**

Trim two forked sticks.

Place sticks along rabbit trail.

Secure wire noose to tree.

Attach noose to sticks.

142 **gut a hare**

Hang and bleed out.

Make incisions in the pelt.

Peel the skin off.

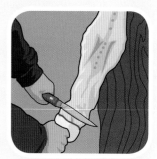
Cut the head off.

Remove the feet and tail.

Slice the abdomen open.

Remove the organs.

Clean the carcass.

squash a squirrel 143

Prop the rock with notched sticks.

Lean a heavy rock on the top stick.

Bait the bottom stick.

nab a fox 144

Tie a rope to the tree, then wrap it around the linchpin.

Anchor the linchpin with a baited stick.

Set the noose underneath the baited stick.

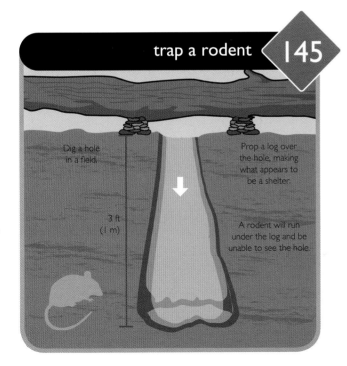

trap a rodent 145

Dig a hole in a field.

Prop a log over the hole, making what appears to be a shelter.

3 ft (1 m)

A rodent will run under the log and be unable to see the hole.

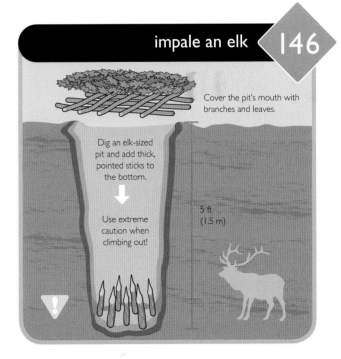

impale an elk 146

Cover the pit's mouth with branches and leaves.

Dig an elk-sized pit and add thick, pointed sticks to the bottom.

Use extreme caution when climbing out!

5 ft (1.5 m)

Pitch your camp in a quiet, open area where you'll be visible to wildlife—and vice versa.

Suspend food out of reach.

If threatened, don't climb up a tree (black bears and some grizzlies can follow you up). Stand still if charged—the bear might be bluffing.

Raise a ruckus and try to make yourself look bigger if a bear approaches.

Do your cooking at least 100 ft (30 m) downwind from the campsite.

Don't leave any food in or near your tent.

pronounced shoulder hump

tall, pointed ears

stubby, rounded ears

flat shoulders

long, flat snout

upturned snout

rounded paw pad with short, thick claws

square-topped paw pad with long, thin claws

black bear

grizzly bear

When it comes to intimidating bears and mountain lions, size does matter. Here are some quick ways to make yourself look bigger.

Hold your jacket over your head.

Wave large, leafy branches.

Have a friend jump on your shoulders.

Face cat; maintain eye contact.

Make noise; wave arms.

Throw rocks if it lunges.

Punch and kick; aim for eyes.

Scare with dominance.

Let go!

Yank the tail to free child.

Kick the ribs.

Move to high ground.

Remove constricting items.

Keep the bite below the heart. Immobilize.

Wash the site with antiseptic soap and water.

Dress with a loose bandage.

Kill the snake.

Bring the snake for identification.

Fend off debilitating jungle eye by looking through the jungle, rather than at individual leaves.

Raise your arms and puff yourself up to appear larger. Slowly back away.

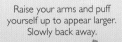

Maintain eye contact.

Think you can outclimb a jungle cat? Think again!

To clear a path, swing a machete in downward strokes. Be careful of your legs!

Don't play dead—you could end up that way!

 +

remove a botfly with bacon **152**

preserve meat in a smoker 37

Note botfly larva.

Wrap area in bacon.

Botfly will burrow out.

Remove bacon.

Behead snake; slit the belly.

Peel off the skin.

Remove the guts.

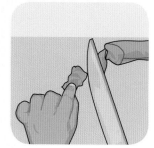

Cut the meat.

To trap a nutritious snake safely, grab a long stick with a fork at the end. Hold the stick just behind the snake's head, then pin it to the ground.

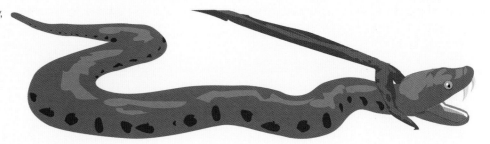

154 eat a scorpion

Stab to hold in place.

Remove stinger.

Skewer.

Roast until brown, crispy.

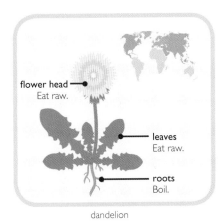

flower head
Eat raw.

leaves
Eat raw.

roots
Boil.

dandelion

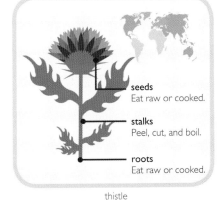

seeds
Eat raw or cooked.

stalks
Peel, cut, and boil.

roots
Eat raw or cooked.

thistle

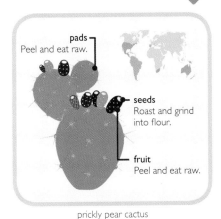

pads
Peel and eat raw.

seeds
Roast and grind
into flour.

fruit
Peel and eat raw.

prickly pear cactus

stems
Wearing gloves,
peel, chop, and
boil or steam.

nettle

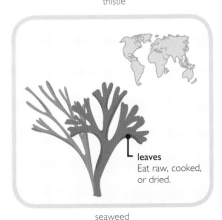

leaves
Eat raw, cooked,
or dried.

seaweed

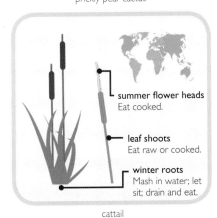

summer flower heads
Eat cooked.

leaf shoots
Eat raw or cooked.

winter roots
Mash in water; let
sit; drain and eat.

cattail

fruit
Eat raw.

heart of palm
Eat raw.

palmetto palm

young pinecones
Boil or bake.

seeds
Dry pinecone;
break open; eat
seeds raw.

new needles
Steep, boil,
or eat raw.

pine tree

flesh
Boil, remove shell,
soak in salt water.

snail

Get warm and dry.

Shield yourself from the sun.

Collect rainwater in a tarp.

See land? Swim to it.

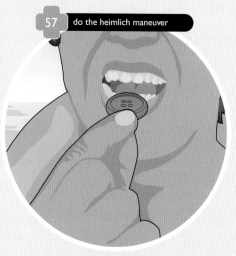

57 do the heimlich maneuver

Suck on a button
to ease thirst.

Remove your pants.

Knot bottoms of the legs.

Pull down to fill with air.

Cinch belt and hug.

If you're adrift at sea and antsy to make landfall, watch for these signs that terra firma is near.

Cumulus clouds gather near solid ground.

Seabirds head away from land during the day and toward it in the evening.

If you see a shape on the horizon, note its color. Land will be green; shadows and clouds will appear gray.

Test the wind: it blows toward land during the day and away at nighttime.

Fields of seaweed grow near land.

You'll spot driftwood from trees (make sure it's not debris from a boat).

Trim limbs from driftwood.

Shape the ends.

Ring the top with mud.

Set fire inside mud ring.

Scrape the charred wood.

Burn; scrape; repeat.

Check for leaks.

Seal leaks with pitch.

161   use coconuts

sunblock
Rub the oil from a mature coconut onto your skin for protection from the tropical sun.

vitamins
Coconut meat, water, and oil are packed with antioxidants, vitamins, and protein.

hydration
The water in young coconuts is full of electrolytes and potassium.

roofing
Use the fronds to to make a shelter.

tableware
Use hollow shells to store liquid or carve them into utensils.

Tie machete to belt.

know your knots 30

Loop a rope around feet.

Grasp trunk.

Bring feet up.

Reach up; bring feet up.

Continue.

Haul machete up.

Cut green coconuts.

palm wine
The sap from palm flowers can be fermented into a wine called toddy.

percussion instruments
Bang empty half-shells together to make music.

rope
Braid coir, the fibrous husk material, into a strong rope.

accessories
Make kitschy jewelry or clothing from the shells.

tinder
Coir and dry leaves help you start a bonfire.

75 treat a jellyfish sting

The pressure drop as you rise to the surface can give you a few more breaths from an "empty" tank.

162 ace an emergency scuba ascent

1 Use tank gauge to confirm that you're out of air.

2 Take last breath if air is available.

3 Calmly kick toward surface.

4 Look up and exhale slowly as you ascend.

If assistance is needed, inflate safety sausage.

Wave to attract help.

Release weight belt if not ascending at normal rate.

escape a kelp forest 163

Check gauges and try breathing normally.

Stay calm.

Use dive knife to cut kelp.

Swim to a clearing.

Crawl along kelp at surface.

Remove shiny jewelry.

Check for open cuts.

Pack a last resort weapon.

Dive during the day.

Stay in a group.

Use controlled movements.

Avoid dolphins and seabirds.

Use air tank to scare sharks.

165 fend off a shark

Yank the gills.

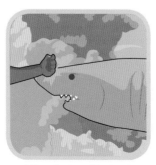

Hit on the top of the head.

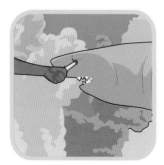

Poke in the eye.

Stab in the face.

Move to solid, dry ground.

tails up

fangs bared

Watch for aggressive stance.

Charge one wolf.

Kick to protect legs.

 Wolves will attack a victim's lower legs in order to bring them down. Kick and shake your legs to repel them.

Avoid direct eye contact.

Climb above dog if possible.

If not, play dead.

rescue-breathe for a dog 102

If attacked, strike eyes.

168 spike an assailant

51 bolt from a wrist grip

Break attacker's grasp.

Put your hand on his head.

Pull his head down.

Follow through.

169 embrace your enemy

Embrace opponent's neck.

Clasp your hands.

Step back; pull neck down.

Straddle and pin arms.

Begin a friendly handshake.

Clasp his forearm.

Spin, holding his forearm.

Grab his bicep.

Pull down abruptly.

Swing him over your shoulder.

Follow thorugh.

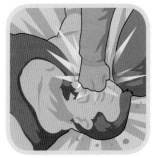

Finish him.

deal with failed brakes

There may be residual pressure left in failed brakes, so go ahead and pump.

24 check a car before a trip

Note failed brakes; stay calm.

Release gas pedal.

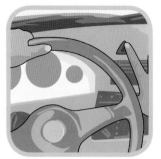

Switch on hazard lights.

Pump brakes.

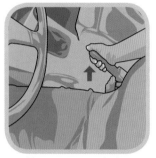

Engage emergency brake.

Downshift if possible.

Nudge car against object.

Exit away from traffic.

172 handle a hydroplaning car

Release gas pedal.

Maintain vehicle direction.

If car turns, turn with it.

Pump after tires reconnect.

 + + +

Cover your nose and mouth.

Run away from the cloud.

Get indoors.

Close windows and doors.

Turn off the thermostat.

Unplug appliances.

Seal openings.

Listen for instructions.

When confronted with a chemical spill, your first task is to get far, far away from it. If you can't reach your hand out and cover the entire accident with your thumb, you're still too close!

It's best to stay off the roads during a snow storm, but if travel can't be avoided, be sure to be safe. Always add additional items like space blankets to your emergency kit.

If your reception is low, try texting for help.

Put on any and all clothing items you might have.

Crack the window and light an emergency candle.

Crumple papers and stuff i clothing for extra warmt

Portion out and eat high-energy foods.

Keep the car turned off.

Don't wander away
from your car.

Make sure to
stretch frequently.

Form a "V" with fingers.

Hold a CD with other hand.

Align object between "V."

Reflect light through "V."

tools

tennis ball   pillow   glass   tarp   cooler   umbrella   radio   pain reliever

bamboo   work glove   cd   change cloth   cool compress   go bag   bacon   rag

plants   snake   bottles   safety shears   bowl   sleeping bag   venison   fire

leaf   ammunition   water   knife   string   scissors   mud   torch

can   hat   syringe   heater   saline solution   fire extinguisher   bucket   safety sausage

branches   hand soap   cornstarch   weight belt   box   id tags and collar   towel   match

canteen   liquid soap   tub   cable lock   sterile gauze   pet go bag   calamine lotion   pet travel cage

 liquid soap

 rfid chip

 pitch

 pelt

cleaning rod

dry tinder

antibiotic cream

 mug

seed

dry leaf

bait

squirrel

iodine

stump

cleanup gear

 rope

hatchet

tent

paper bag

long stick

belt

forked sticks

tinder

plank

 stick

 dog treat

 target

 driftwood

 hydrogen peroxide

 bandage

 extra padding

 shoes

 charred wood

 leaves

 large box

 logs

 oiled cloth

 shell

 moleskin

 elastic bandage

 fishing stick

 cardboard

 sandbags

 thread

 seasonings

 baking soda

 sand

 cloth pads

 syrup of ipecac

 broom

 empty sandbag

 fire setup

 chocolate

 sock

 map

 rubber gloves

 forked branch

 credit card

 key safe

 photo

 twine

 avalanche beacon

 powdered ginger

mug of water

fish hook · paper towel · ice · antiviral medicine · ice chisel · water bowl · button · fishing line

hardwood stick · pen · rubbing alcohol · needle · machete · box cutter · rock · knife

sticks · cloth · resealable bags · spoon · shovel · snow probe · scorpion · eyedropper

string · tissue paper · thermometer · diving knife · mini emergency kit · inhaler · lighter · milk

candle · soap · tape · newspaper · duct tape · tweezers · blanket · pan

airtight bandage · gauze · air tank · hazard pamphlet · thermos · dead rabbit · bucket of water · gun

butterfly strips · ice cubes · foil · gun safes · pet food and water · shovel · mobile phones · jacket

cotton swab · jar · pet food · padding · gun case · pants · wire · scuba gear

index

139

47

5

147

174

6

25

35

150

76

22

153

99

151

166

show me who

weldon**owen**

415 Jackson Street
San Francisco CA 94111
www.wopublishing.com

CEO, President Terry Newell

VP, Sales and
New Business Development Amy Kaneko

VP, Publisher Roger Shaw

Associate Creative Director Kelly Booth

Executive Editor Mariah Bear

Editor Lucie Parker

Project Editors Frances Reade, Jann Jones

Editorial Assistant Emelie Griffin

Senior Designer Stephanie Tang

Designers Meghan Hildebrand, Rachel Liang

Illustration Coordinator Conor Buckley

Production Director Chris Hemesath

Production Manager Michelle Duggan

Production Coordinator Charles Mathews

Color Manager Teri Bell

OUTDOORLIFE

2 Park Avenue
New York NY 10016
www.outdoorlife.com

Editor-in-Chief Todd Smith

VP, Group Publisher Eric Zinczenko

Senior Managing Editor Camille Rankin

Senior Editor John Taranto

Outdoor Life and Weldon Owen are divisions of
BONNIER

Library of Congress Control Number is on file
with the publisher.

Paperback ISBN: 978-1-61628-132-8
Hardcover ISBN: 978-1-61628-177-9

10 9 8 7 6 5 4 3 2
2014 2013 2012 2011

Printed in China by 1010

Weldon Owen would like to thank:

Storyboarders
Sarah Duncan, Sheila Masson, Jamie Spinello,
Brandi Valenza, Astrea White, Kevin Yuen

Illustration specialists
Hayden Foell, Jamie Spinello, Ross Sublett

Editorial and research support team
Alex Eros, Marianna Monaco, Katharine Moore,
Gail Nelson-Bonebrake, Camille Rankin, Paula
Rogers, Marisa Solís, John Taranto, Mary Zhang

Special thanks to Kemi Ando for her in-depth
research and support on this title.

A **Show Me Now** Book.
Show Me Now is a trademark
of Weldon Owen Inc.
www.showmenow.com

ILLUSTRATION CREDITS The artwork in this book
was a true team effort. We are happy to thank and
acknowledge our illustrators.

Front Cover: Juan Calle: scorpion, ice hole rescue
Bryon Thompson: flashlight

Back Cover: Juan Calle: sandbags, spike assailant
Joshua Kemble: sling

Key bg=background, fr=frames

Steve Baletsa: 2, 3, 4, 23, 51, 65, 66, 92, 93, 94 Juan
Calle (Liberum Donum): 1, 15, 16, 17, 18, 19, 22, 26, 31
fr, 32 fr, 33 fr, 34 fr, 35, 38, 39, 41, 45, 48, 49, 52, 53, 59,
70, 75, 80, 82, 83, ,96, 97, 98, 99, 104, 105, 106, 107,
108, 109, 112, 113, 134, 135, 136, 137, 148 149, 162,
163, 164, 165, 166, 167, 168, 169, 170, 171, 172, 174,
175 Hayden Foell: 5, 6, 7, 8, 9, 25, 40, 44, 67, 69, 120,
121, 122, 123, 129, 139, 143, 144, 145, 146, 152 Britt
Hanson: 10, 31 bg, 32 bg, 33 bg, 34 bg, 47, 147 Joshua
Kemble: 56, 57, 63, 64, 68, 74, 77, 81, 86, 91, 95,138,

139, 141, 142, 153, 156, 173 Vic Kulihin: 157
Raymond Larrett: 13, 24, 101, 102, 103, 124, 125, 126,
154, 159 Christine Meighan: 30 Vincent Perea: 110,
111,140, 150, 151 Jamie Spinello: 36, 87, 88, 89, 90,
160, 161 Bryon Thompson: 60, 61, 62, 85, 116, 117,
118, 119, 127, 128, 130, 131, 132, 133 Lauren Towner:
11, 12, 71, 73, 100 Gabhor Utomo: 14, 20, 21, 27, 28,
29, 30 fr, 54, 76, 84, 114, 158 Tina Cash Walsh: 46, 58,
115 Paul Williams 50 Mary Zins: 37, 42, 43, 78, 79

a final note

Now that you've read this book, you're ready to go out there and make the world a better place (#104), or at least take care of yourself and help your friends and loved ones (#19). If you want to keep learning about first aid and survival, look into taking some classes, doing volunteer work (#103), and reaching out to your community (#35). The positive mindset and skills you've learned will take you far.

about *Outdoor Life*

Outdoor Life (OutdoorLife.com) is the source for hunting and fishing adventure and one of American's leading outdoor publications. Founded in 1898, *Outdoor Life* provides technical information, survival tips, wilderness destinations, field reports and gear guides for hands-on outdoor enthusiasts.

hey, you!

Is there something that you think should have been in this book? Do you have an amazing skill you want to share with the world? Is there something we didn't get quite right? Send us your ideas, feedback, or even photos or video of you demonstrating your sweet skills (nothing dangerous, kids), and you could be featured in the next Show Me Now book.

 www.showmenow.com

 ATTN: SHOW ME TEAM
Weldon Owen Inc.
415 Jackson Street
San Francisco, California 94111